**TEACHER'S PET PUBLICATIONS**

LITPLAN TEACHER PACK
for
The Effect of Gamma Rays on
Man in the Moon Marigolds
based on the book by
Paul Zindel

Written by
Marion B. Hoffman

© 1999 Teacher's Pet Publications
All Rights Reserved

This **LitPlan** for Paul Zindel's
The Effect of Gamma Rays on Man-in-the-Moon Marigolds
has been brought to you by Teacher's Pet Publications, Inc.

Copyright Teacher's Pet Publications 1999

Only the student materials in this unit plan
such as worksheets, study questions, assignment sheets, and tests
may be reproduced multiple times for use in the purchaser's classroom.

For any additional copyright questions,
contact Teacher's Pet Publications.

www.tpet.com

TABLE OF CONTENTS
The Effects of Gamma Rays on Man-in-the-Moon Marigolds

Introduction	6
Unit Objectives	9
Reading Assignment Sheet	10
Unit Outline	11
Study Questions (Short Answer)	15
Quiz/Study Questions (Multiple Choice)	25
Pre-reading Vocabulary Worksheets	45
Lesson One (Introductory Lesson)	57
Nonfiction Assignment Sheet	59
Oral Reading Evaluation Form	60
Writing Assignment #1	66
Writing Assignment #2	72
Writing Assignment #3	74
Vocabulary Review Activities	83
Extra Writing Assignments/Discussion ?s	79
Unit Review Activities	85
Unit Tests	89
Unit Resource Materials	113
Vocabulary Resource Materials	129

A Few Notes About The Author - Paul Zindel

Paul Zindel is an author who understands and enjoys his audience. Not only does he say in interviews that he likes teenagers and feels a special proclivity for them and their lives, but again and again his voice speaks out for teenagers in his books. He has a sense of fun and authenticity about him that young people seem almost universally to respond favorably to.

Zindel was born on Staten Island in New York City in 1936. About the time that he was two years old, his father left the family. Zindel was raised by a single mother.

The fact that they were forced to move a great deal during his childhood may have deprived him of some of the close relationships that children often form. But having so many experiences so young apparently provided him with a storehouse of knowledge gained by observing situations and people along the way. According to Zindel himself, all of his books started with some experience in his own life.

After attending public elementary school in New York, he went on to Port Richmond High School in the same city. It was there that he published his first story collaboratively with a schoolmate. "A Geometric Nightmare" was, not surprisingly, a story that describes a geometry teacher who frightened Zindel and the other student.

Zindel graduated from Wagner College and became a high school chemistry teacher. He taught for ten years before his play, *The Effect of Gamma Rays on Man-in-the-Moon Marigolds* was produced in 1965. At that point he began to dedicate full time to his writing.

Zindel currently lives in Manhattan. He is married and the father of two post-teenage children. He has always had a variety of pets in his life.

Some of Zindel's most noteworthy works, in addition to *Gamma Rays*, for which he won the 1971 Pulitzer Prize and the New York Critics Circle Award, are **The Pigman** (1968), **My Darling, My Hamburger** (1969), **I Never Loved Your Mind** (1970), **Pardon Me, You're Stepping on My Eyeball** (1976), **Confessions of a Teenage Baboon** (1977), **The Undertaker's Gone Bananas** (1978), **The Pigman's Legacy** (1980), **Harry and Hortense at Hormone High** (1984), and **The Amazing and Death-Defying Diary of Eugene Dingman** (1987).

The Bantam paperback edition of **The Effect of Gamma Rays on Man-in-the-Moon Marigolds** used for this unit plan quotes *Variety* on the play's success: "Paul Zindel has written a masterful, pacesetting drama. It combines moments of pain, poignancy, beauty and hope. It is the most compelling work of its kind since Tennessee Williams *The Glass Menagerie*."

A Few Notes About the Author continued page 2

In the same paperback, twenty-five years after *Marigolds* was first published and produced, Zindel writes:

> *I can't help being reminded of my favorite theory: We all, most basically, create and tell stories to solve problems. We conjure all sorts of strange characters, march them into frantic conflict with each other, and, at the end of the battle, hope we've learned something. It's important, too, that those who read and hear our stories find answers for their own lives. We look for insights, epiphanies, that shed light on humanness, tolerance, anguish, and compassion. We want to glimpse who we really are and understand why we're on this planet. And, of course, we writers write in dreamlike codes, do anything to throw our readers off the track, praying no one will catch on that we are putting on display little pieces of our joys, our fears, and our hearts.*

The characters in *Marigolds* are based on Zindel's mother and sister, and even, a little bit, in the person of Tillie, on himself. It will be worthwhile to read some introductory material on Paul Zindel and his life. Some of that information may be found in Zindel's autobiography, **The Pigman and Me**, and in various introductions to his works. A great deal is also available about Zindel on the internet. Interested readers can even hear a recording of the author's voice. This is a most accessible writer.

INTRODUCTION

This unit has been designed to develop students' reading, writing, thinking, and language skills through exercises and activities related to **The Effect of Gamma Rays on Man-in-the-Moon Marigolds** by Paul Zindel. It includes nineteen lessons, supported by extra resource materials.

The **introductory lesson** introduces students to one theme of the play: dreams through a bulletin board activity. Subsequent lessons allow for discussion of additional themes and ideas.

The **reading assignments** are very short because the play itself is made up of only two relatively short acts. Students have approximately 15 minutes of pre-reading work to do prior to each reading assignment. This pre-reading work involves reviewing the study questions for the assignment and doing some vocabulary work for 7 to 10 vocabulary words they will encounter in their reading. You may want to have students do the vocabulary work as they read each section.

The **study guide questions** are fact-based; students can find the answers to these questions right in the text. These questions come in two formats: short answer or multiple choice. The best use of these materials is probably to use the short answer version of the questions as study guides for students since answers will be more complete and to use the multiple choice version for occasional quizzes.

The **vocabulary work** is intended to enrich students' vocabularies as well as to aid in the students' understanding of the book. Prior to each reading assignment, students will complete a two-part worksheet for approximately 7 to 10 vocabulary words in the upcoming reading assignment. Part I focuses on students' use of general knowledge and contextual clues by giving the sentence in which the word appears in the text. Students are then to write down what they think the words mean based on the words' usage. Part II nails down the definitions of the words by giving students dictionary definitions of the words and having students match the words to the correct definitions based on the words' contextual usage. Students should then have a good understanding of the words when they meet them in the text.

After each reading assignment, students will go back and formulate answers for the study guide questions. Discussion of these questions serves as a **review** of the most important events and ideas presented in the reading assignments.

After students complete extra discussion questions, there is a **vocabulary review** lesson which pulls together all of the fragmented vocabulary lists for the reading assignments and gives students a review of all of the words they have studied.

Marigolds Introduction page 2

Following the reading of the play, two lessons are devoted to the **extra discussion questions/writing assignments**. These questions focus on interpretation, critical analysis, and personal response, employing a variety of thinking skills and adding to the students' understanding of the novel. These questions may be done as a **group activity**. Using the information they have acquired so far through individual work and class discussions, students may get together to further examine the text and to brainstorm ideas relating to the themes of the novel.

Throughout the unit students are given the opportunity to read aloud, make classroom presentations, lead discussion, and make updates on work they are doing. Thus students get to practice working in a variety of ways and the whole class gets to hear different ideas relative to the play they are reading.

There are three **writing assignments** in this unit, each with the purpose of informing, persuading, or expressing personal opinions. The first assignment is to inform: students build on the work that they have done for the Nonfiction Reading Assignment and write about an aspect of starting a new business. This assignment helps students to consider what is involved in starting and maintaining a new business The second assignment gives students the opportunity to express their personal ideas: students get to tell about their most important personal dream. This assignment will help students to draw conclusions from the play's events and to examine the characters and their dreams more closely. The third assignment is to give students a chance to persuade: students choose and write about a character in the play. This assignment helps them to distinguish between characters, to define their terms, and to examine one character in depth.

In addition, there is a **nonfiction reading assignment**. Students are required to read a piece of nonfiction related in some way to **Marigolds**. After reading their nonfiction pieces, students will fill out a worksheet on which they answer questions regarding facts, interpretation, criticism, and personal opinions. If you have time to allow individual students to make **oral presentations** about the nonfiction pieces they have read, the whole class will be exposed to a wealth of information and students will also have the opportunity to practice public speaking.

There is an optional **class project** (Project New Business) through which students gain first-hand knowledge of the growing trend of people starting their own businesses.

The **review lesson** pulls together all aspects of the unit. The teacher is given four or five choices of activities or games to use which all serve the same basic function of reviewing all of the information presented in the unit.

Marigolds Introduction page 3

The five **unit tests** come in three separate formats:
matching/short answer/essay/vocabulary (2 tests)
matching/short answer critical thinking/quotations/vocabulary (1 advanced test)
matching/multiple choice/essay/vocabulary (2 tests)

Also in this unit is an **extra activities packet** with suggestions for an in-class library, crossword and word search puzzles related to **Marigolds**, and extra vocabulary worksheets. There is a list of **bulletin board ideas** which gives suggestions for bulletin boards to go along with this unit. In addition, there is a list of **extra class activities** the teacher could use to enhance the unit or as a substitution for an exercise the teacher feels is inappropriate for his or her class.

Answer keys are located directly after the **reproducible student materials** throughout the unit. The student materials may be reproduced for use in the teacher's classroom without infringement of copyright. No other portion of this unit may be reproduced without the written consent of Teacher's Pet Publications, Inc.

UNIT OBJECTIVES
The Effect of Gamma Rays on Man-in-the-Moon Marigolds

1. Through reading **The Effect of Gamma Rays on Man-in-the-Moon Marigolds** by Paul Zindel, students will gain a better understanding of the themes of trust, family responsibility, community values, and the responsibilities of pet ownership. One theme, pet ownership, is focused on specifically.

2. Students will demonstrate their understanding of the text on four levels: factual, interpretive, critical, and personal.

3. Students will define their own viewpoints on the aforementioned themes.

4. Students will be exposed to new ways of looking at the themes above.

5. Students will create a plan for solving some of the problems created by irresponsible pet ownership.

6. Students will practice reading aloud as well as silently.

7. Students will enrich their vocabularies and improve their understanding of the novel through the vocabulary lessons prepared for use in conjunction with it.

8. Students will practice writing through a variety of assignments.

9. The writing assignments in this unit are geared to several purposes:
    a. to check the students' reading comprehension
    b. to make students think about the ideas presented in the book
    c. to allow students to write from personal experience, to inform, and to persuade
    d. to provide the opportunity to review standard English
    e. to encourage critical and logical thinking

10. Students will be encouraged to make connections between the book and real life.

READING ASSIGNMENT SHEET
The Effect of Gamma Rays on Man-in-the-Moon Marigolds

Date Assigned	Reading Assignment	Completion Date
	Section 1	
	Section 2	
	Section 3	
	Section 4	
	Section 5	
	Section 6	
	Section 7	
	Section 8	
	Section 9	

UNIT OUTLINE
The Effect of Gamma Rays on Man-in-the-Moon Marigolds

1	2	3	4	5
Read Zindel Essay Introduction Theme Discussion	PVR Section 1 Read "The Setting" PVR Section 2	Review Section 1 Review Section 2 Practice Reading Dialogue	Review Section 2 PVR Section 3 Nonfiction Reading Assignment	Review Section 3 Writing Assign. 1
6	**7**	**8**	**9**	**10**
PVR Section 4 Character Exercise	Project New Business	Review Section 4 PVR Section 5 Project	Writing Assign. 2	Review Section 5 PVR Section 6
11	**12**	**13**	**14**	**15**
Review Section 6 PVR Section 7 Writing Assign. 3	Role Playing	Review Section 7 PVR Section 8	Review Section 8 PVR Section 9	Review Extra Discussion ?s
16	**17**	**18**	**19**	
Finish Discussions	Vocabulary Review	Unit Review	Unit Test	

Key: P = Preview Study Questions   V = Vocabulary Work   R = Read

STUDY GUIDE QUESTIONS AND ANSWER KEY

SHORT ANSWER STUDY QUESTIONS
The Effect of Gamma Rays on Man-in-the-Moon Marigolds

Section 1: From the first sound of Tillie's voice until Beatrice tells her "Then shut up."
1. What part of her body does Tillie say came partially from a star?
2. What was the small thing that Tillie says existed from the beginning of the world?
3. Whose voice is first heard while the character is still off stage?
4. What two words does Beatrice use to describe Mr. Goodman while she is on the phone with him?
5. What does Beatrice say is the worst thing in this modern world?
6. What is the first word that Beatrice uses to describe Mr. Goodman once she is off the phone with him?
7. On what does Tillie say that Mr. Goodman is going to do an experiment?
8. Why won't Beatrice let Tillie go to school?
9. What is Tillie's real first name?

Section 2: From Ruth's first appearance until the stage goes to dark and music begins
1. What impression does Ruth give right from the beginning?
2. What does Ruth say Tillie did the day before to make the other students laugh at her?
3. How does Ruth describe Tillie's outfit and her hair?
4. What two things do Ruth and Beatrice share in the morning?
5. What does Ruth do for Beatrice while she tells her about Tillie?
6. What is **the history** that Ruth refers to?
7. What is Ruth's favorite brand of cigarettes?

Section 3: From Tillie's second speech envisioning her science project to just prior to Nanny's entrance
1. In her vision, what does Tillie remember seeing behind the glass?
2. What does Tillie say would happen to the fountain?
3. When the lights come up, what is Tillie doing with her seeds?
4. What kind of seeds are they?
5. What have the seeds been exposed to?
6. What are two programs that Beatrice admits she never finished?
7. What new business does Beatrice say she is thinking of going into?

Section 4: From Nanny's rustling at the curtains to the set's going dark after Beatrice talks about her "half-lifes"
1. What is the first evidence seen of Nanny?
2. What can be seen in Nanny's eyes?
3. What does Nanny's shuffling motion remind one of?
4. How does Beatrice speak to Nanny?
5. What is the difference between what Beatrice actually says to Nanny in capital letters and what she is thinking in lower case letters?
6. What does Beatrice say Nanny's daughter is pretending to be?
7. What one mistake does Beatrice say caused her downfall?

Marigolds Short Answer Study Questions continued page 2

8. What does Beatrice say she thinks she will do when Nanny's daughter comes to visit her mother again?
9. How does Beatrice say she is going to kill the rabbit?
10. What is Nanny's "duty"?

Section 5: From the sound of Beatrice's dialing the phone until she hangs up from talking with Mr. Goodman

1. Who is Beatrice trying to call?
2. What is Beatrice's last name?
3. What job is Ruth doing for Mr. Goodman?
4. What are three of Ruth's duties in her job with Mr. Goodman?
5. Why is Beatrice worried about Tillie's seeds?
6. What two things is Beatrice doing while she talks with Mr. Goodman on the phone?

Section 6: From the time that the music rises to thunder crashes until the stage goes dark after Beatrice tells Ruth about her nightmare

1. Who screams at the beginning of this section?
2. How does Beatrice divert Ruth's attention from her fright and make her laugh?
3. When the electricity goes off, what does Beatrice look for right away?
4. What man is Ruth supposedly so afraid of?
5. What story does Ruth want Beatrice to tell her?
6. What had Beatrice done with her father's wagon years ago?
7. What part of Beatrice's story doesn't Ruth want to hear?
8. Where are Beatrice's parents now?
9. Whose face does Beatrice see in the window in her own nightmare?

Section 7: From the time the lights come on Nanny at the kitchen table with the beer in front of her until the music starts and the lights fade after Tillie cries-**END OF ACT I**

1. Why does Beatrice say she hasn't killed the rabbit?
2. What does Beatrice say she came up with when she took stock of her life?
3. What news does Beatrice tell about Tillie?
4. Who calls Beatrice on the phone and what does he want her to do?
5. How does Beatrice react to Dr. Berg's invitation?
6. Who does Beatrice say she would look like up on the stage?
7. What does Beatrice do when Tillie begins to cry?

Marigolds Short Answer Study Questions continued page 3

Section 8: From the **BEGINNING OF ACT II** about two weeks later until Beatrice breaks into tears and decides not to go to the fair

1. What is Tillie preparing to do at the beginning of Act II?
2. What is the main title on the large screen that stands on one of the tables?
3. What is the subtopic on the screen?
4. Who does Ruth say is Tillie's only competition at the fair?
5. What item of Tillie's clothing does Ruth say will make people laugh?
6. According to Ruth, how did Mr. Goodman say Beatrice sounded over the phone?
7. According to Ruth, what did Miss Hanley say Beatrice's nickname used to be?
8. What did Janice Vickery boil in a pot of water?
9. Who is the boy that Ruth worries about being embarrassed in front of?
10. Why does Tillie give her rabbit to Ruth?
11. What does Tillie say about Beatrice's appearance when Beatrice appears at the top of the stairs all dressed up?
12. What does Beatrice say happens to people who are just a little bit different in this world?
13. Why won't Beatrice let Ruth go along to school with her and Tillie?
14. What does Beatrice say she feels in the back of her brain?
15. What does Ruth call Beatrice just as Beatrice starts to go out the door to get in the taxi?

Section 9: From the beginning of Janice's presentation to the **END OF THE PLAY**

1. Where does Janice say she got the cat for her experiment?
2. What does Janice say she boiled the cat in?
3. What does Janice do between parts of her presentation?
4. What is Beatrice doing as the spotlight comes up on her?
5. What message does Beatrice leave on the phone for Dr. Berg, Mr. Goodman, and Miss Hanley?
6. Who does Beatrice call next?
7. What does Beatrice tell Nanny's daughter?
8. What has Beatrice done to the rabbit while Tillie and Ruth were gone?
9. Why doesn't Beatrice want to call the doctor when Ruth has another episode?
10. What does Beatrice tell Tillie she hates?
11. What does Tillie say is the most important thing her experiment has done?

KEY: SHORT ANSWER STUDY QUESTIONS
The Effect of Gamma Rays on Man-in-the-Moon Marigolds

Section 1: From the first sound of Tillie's voice until Beatrice tells her "Then shut up."

1. What part of her body does Tillie say came partially from a star?
   She says her hand came partially from a star.

2. What was the small thing that Tillie says existed from the beginning of the world?
   The small thing was an atom.

3. Whose voice is first heard while the character is still off stage?
   Beatrice's voice is first heard while her character is still off stage.

4. What two words does Beatrice use to describe Mr. Goodman while she is on the phone with him?
   Beatrice describes Mr. Goodman as delightful and handsome.

5. What does Beatrice say is the worst thing in this modern world?
   She says strain is the worst thing in this modern world.

6. What is the first word that Beatrice uses to describe Mr. Goodman once she is off the phone with him?
   She says he is ugly.

7. On what does Tillie say that Mr. Goodman is going to do an experiment?
   She says he is going to do an experiment on radioactivity.

8. Why won't Beatrice let Tillie go to school?
   Beatrice won't let her go to school because she wants her to help at home.

9. What is Tillie's real first name?
   Tillie's real first name is Matilda.

Section 2: From Ruth's first appearance until the stage goes to dark and music begins

1. What impression does Ruth give right from the beginning?
   Ruth gives the impression of being slightly strange.

2. What does Ruth say Tillie did the day before to make the other students laugh at her?
   She demonstrated a model of an atom at a school assembly.

3. How does Ruth describe Tillie's outfit and her hair?
   She says she was wearing an old jumper with a raggy slip and had lightning hair.

Marigolds Key: Short Answer Study Questions continued page 2

4. What two things do Ruth and Beatrice share in the morning?
   Ruth and Beatrice share lipstick and cigarettes.

5. What does Ruth do for Beatrice while she tells her about Tillie?
   Ruth scratches Beatrice's back with a backscratcher.

6. What is **the history** that Ruth refers to?
   It is the story of her family's lives kept by the school.

7. What is Ruth's favorite brand of cigarettes?
   Ruth's favorite brand of cigarettes is Kools.

Section 3: From Tillie's second speech envisioning her science project to just prior to Nanny's entrance

1. In her vision, what does Tillie remember seeing behind the glass?
   She saw a white cloud beginning to form.

2. What does Tillie say would happen to the fountain of smoke?
   She says it would go on for millions of years.

3. When the lights come up, what is Tillie doing with her seeds?
   Tillie is planting her seeds.

4. What kind of seeds are they?
   They are marigold seeds.

5. What have the seeds been exposed to?
   The seeds have been exposed to cobalt-60.

6. What are two programs that Beatrice admits she never finished?
   She never finished the real estate course or beauty school.

7. What new business does Beatrice say she is thinking of going into?
   She says she is thinking of opening up a tea shop.

Section 4: From Nanny's rustling at the curtains to the set's going dark after Beatrice talks about her "half-lifes"

1. What is the first evidence seen of Nanny?
   The first evidence seen of Nanny is her thin and wrinkled hands.

2. What can be seen in Nanny's eyes?
   Great cataracts can be seen in Nanny's eyes.

Marigolds Key: Short Answer Study Questions continued page 3

3. What does Nanny's shuffling motion remind one of?
   Nanny's shuffling motion reminds one of a ticking clock.

4. How does Beatrice speak to Nanny?
   Beatrice speaks to Nanny as though the old woman were a deaf year-old child.

5. What is the difference between what Beatrice actually says to Nanny in capital letters and what she is thinking in lower case letters?
   In capital letters Beatrice speaks nicely to Nanny, but in lower case letters she says what she is really thinking.

6. What does Beatrice say Nanny's daughter is pretending to be?
   Beatrice says Nanny's daughter is pretending to be Miss Career Woman of the Year.

7. What one mistake does Beatrice say started her downfall?
   Beatrice says her downfall started when she married the wrong man and got tied down with children.

8. What does Beatrice say she thinks she will do when Nanny's daughter comes to visit her mother again?
   Beatrice says she thinks she will drop dead.

9. How does Beatrice say she is going to kill the rabbit?
   Beatrice says she is going to chloroform the rabbit.

10. What is Nanny's "duty"?
    Nanny's "duty" is going to the bathroom.

<u>Section 5: From the sound of Beatrice's dialing the phone until she hangs up from talking with Mr. Goodman</u>

1. Who is Beatrice trying to call on the phone?
   Beatrice is trying to call Mr. Goodman.

2. What is Beatrice's last name?
   Beatrice's last name is Hunsdorfer.

3. What job is Ruth doing for Mr. Goodman?
   Ruth is acting as Mr. Goodman's secretary.

4. What are three of Ruth's duties in her job with Mr. Goodman?
   Three of Ruth's duties are keeping attendance, taking care of the cut cards, and typing.

Marigolds Key: Short Answer Study Questions continued page 4

5. Why is Beatrice worried about Tillie's seeds?
   Beatrice is worried about Tillie's seeds being radioactive.

6. What two things is Beatrice doing while she talks with Mr. Goodman on the phone?
   While Beatrice talks with Mr. Goodman, she laughs and smokes a cigarette.

Section 6: From the time that the music rises to thunder crashes until the stage goes dark after Beatrice tells Ruth about her nightmare

1. Who screams at the beginning of this section?
   Ruth screams at the beginning of this section.

2. How does Beatrice divert Ruth's attention from her fright and make her laugh?
   She makes a comic face for Ruth.

3. When the electricity goes off, what does Beatrice look for right away?
   She looks for the little candles that were on her last year's birthday cake.

4. What is the name of the man Ruth is supposedly so afraid of?
   The man's name is Mr. Mayo.

5. What story does Ruth want Beatrice to tell her?
   Ruth wants Beatrice to tell her the story of the wagon.

6. What had Beatrice done with her father's wagon years ago?
   Beatrice got into her father's wagon and drove it herself.

7. What part of Beatrice's story doesn't Ruth want to hear?
   Ruth doesn't want to hear about the dead horses.

8. Where are Beatrice's parents now?
   Beatrice's parents are both deceased.

9. Whose face does Beatrice see in the window in her own nightmare?
   Beatrice sees her dead father's face in the window.

Section 7: From the time the lights come on Nanny at the kitchen table with the beer in front of her until the music starts and the lights fade after Tillie cries-**END OF ACT I**

1. Why does Beatrice say she hasn't killed the rabbit?
   She says she hasn't killed the rabbit because Ruth would have convulsions for fifty years as a result.

Marigolds Key: Short Answer Study Questions continued page 5

2. What does Beatrice say she came up with when she took stock of her life?
   Beatrice says she came up with "zero."

3. What news does Ruth tell Beatrice about Tillie?
   Ruth tells Beatrice that Tillie is one of the finalists in a science fair.

4. Who calls Beatrice on the phone and what does he want her to do?
   Dr. Berg, the school principal, calls Beatrice to invite her to sit on the stage with the mothers of the other science fair finalists.

5. How does Beatrice react to Dr. Berg's invitation?
   She tells Dr. Berg that she will think about it.

6. Who does Beatrice say she would look like up on the stage?
   She says she would look like Tillie.

7. What does Beatrice do when Tillie begins to cry?
   She embraces her.

Section 8: From the **BEGINNING OF ACT II** about two weeks later until Beatrice breaks into tears and decides not to go to the fair

1. What is Tillie preparing to do at the beginning of Act II?
   Tillie is preparing to take her science project to the final judging of the science fair.

2. What is the main title on the large screen that stands on one of the tables?
   THE EFFECT OF GAMMA RAYS ON MAN-IN-THE-MOON MARIGOLDS.

3. What is the subtopic on the screen?
   THE PAST; THE PRESENT; THE FUTURE.

4. Who does Ruth say is Tillie's only competition at the fair?
   Ruth says Tillie's only competition is Janice Vickery.

5. What item of Tillie's clothing does Ruth say will make people laugh?
   Ruth says Tillie's hair bow will make people laugh.

6. According to Ruth, how did Mr. Goodman say Beatrice sounded over the phone?
   According to Ruth, Mr. Goodman said that Beatrice sounded crazy.

7. According to Ruth, what did Miss Hanley say Beatrice's nickname used to be?
   According to Ruth, Miss Hanley said Beatrice's nickname used to be **Betty the Loon**.

Marigolds Key: Short Answer Study Questions continued page 6

8. What did Janice Vickery boil in a pot?
   Janice boiled a cat in a pot.

9. Who is the boy that Ruth worries about being embarrassed in front of?
   Ruth is worried about being embarrassed in front of Chris Burns.

10. Why does Tillie give her rabbit to Ruth?
    Tillie gives her rabbit to Ruth in exchange for Ruth's agreeing not to tell Beatrice that people are laughing at her.

11. What does Tillie say about Beatrice's appearance when Beatrice appears at the top of the stairs all dressed up?
    Tillie says, "Mama, you look beautiful."

12. What does Beatrice say happens to people who are just a little bit different in this world?
    She says that people try to kill them off.

13. Why won't Beatrice let Ruth go along to school with her and Tillie?
    Beatrice won't let Ruth go along because someone has to stay home to care for Nanny.

14. What does Beatrice say she feels in the back of her brain?
    She says that in the back of her brain she feels just a little *proud*.

15. What does Ruth call Beatrice just as Beatrice starts to go out the door to get in the taxi?
    Ruth calls Beatrice "Betty the Loon."

Section 9: From the beginning of Janice's presentation to the **END OF THE PLAY**
1. Where does Janice say she got the cat for her experiment?
   Janice says she got the cat from the ASPCA.

2. What does Janice say she boiled the cat in?
   She says she boiled it in a sodium hydroxide solution.

3. What does Janice do between parts of her presentation?
   In between parts of her presentation, Janice laughs.

4. What is Beatrice doing as the spotlight comes up on her?
   She is going through a phone book.

Marigolds Key: Short Answer Study Questions continued page 7

5. What has Beatrice obviously been doing?
   Beatrice obviously has been drinking.

6. What message does Beatrice leave on the phone for Dr. Berg, Mr. Goodman, and Miss Hanley?
   She says to thank them for making her wish she was dead.

6. Who does Beatrice call next?
   Next Beatrice calls Nanny's daughter.

7. What does Beatrice tell Nanny's daughter?
   Beatrice tells Nanny's daughter to come and get her mother by the next day.

8. What has Beatrice done to the rabbit while Tillie and Ruth were gone?
   While Tillie and Ruth were gone, Beatrice killed the rabbit.

9. Why doesn't Beatrice want to call the doctor when Ruth has another episode?
   She doesn't want to call the doctor because she wants to keep her money for setting up a business.

10. What does Beatrice tell Tillie she hates?
    Beatrice tells Tillie she hates the world.

11. What does Tillie say is the most important thing her experiment has done?
    Tillie says her experiment has made her feel important.

MULTIPLE CHOICE QUIZZES
The Effect of Gamma Rays on Man-in-the-Moon Marigolds

Section 1: From the first sound of Tillie's voice until Beatrice tells her "Then shut up."

1. What part of her body does Tillie say came partially from a star?
    a. Her head
    b. Her heart
    c. Her hand
    d. Her feet

2. What was the small thing that Tillie says existed from the beginning of the world?
    a. Hope
    b. God
    c. Mankind
    d. An atom

3. Whose voice is first heard while the character is still off stage?
    a. Beatrice's
    b. Miss Hanley's
    c. Nanny's
    d. The rabbit's

4. What two words does Beatrice use to describe Mr. Goodman while she is on the phone with him?
    a. True and honorable
    b. Smart and tall
    c. Delightful and handsome
    d. Short and ugly

5. What does Beatrice say is the worst thing in this modern world?
    a. Loss of true love
    b. Strain
    c. Disappointment
    d. Lack of courage

6. What is the first word that Beatrice uses to describe Mr. Goodman once she is off the phone with him?
    a. Gorgeous
    b. Friendly
    c. Intelligent
    d. Ugly

Marigolds Multiple Choice Quizzes continued page 2

7. On what does Tillie say that Mr. Goodman is going to do an experiment?
    a. People's ability to withstand strain
    b. Stress in life
    c. Radioactivity
    d. Phases of the moon

8. Why won't Beatrice let Tillie go to school?
    a. Because she knows Tillie doesn't do well in school
    b. Because if Ruth can't go, neither can Tillie
    c. Because she wants Tillie to help her at home
    d. Because Tillie prefers not to go anyway

9. What is Tillie's real first name?
    a. Tilliman
    b. Tillicent
    c. Matilda
    d. Millicent

Marigolds Multiple Choice Quizzes continued page 3

Section 2: From Ruth's first appearance until the stage goes to dark and music begins

1. What impression does Ruth give right from the beginning?
    a. Of being a really smart girl
    b. Of being much younger than she is
    c. Of being much older than she is
    d. Of being slightly strange

2. What does Ruth say Tillie did the day before to make the other students laugh at her?
    a. She danced in the halls.
    b. She demonstrated a model of an atom at a school assembly.
    c. She sang in front of the entire student body.
    d. She went to school without any shoes on.

3. How does Ruth describe Tillie's outfit and her hair?
    a. She says she was wearing an old jumper with a raggy slip and had lightning hair.
    b. She says she was wearing a too-short jumper and her hair wasn't combed.
    c. She says she was wearing the wrong color jumper and had a big bow in her hair.
    d. She says she wasn't wearing a bra and her hair bow had slipped way down on her head.

4. What two things do Ruth and Beatrice share in the morning?
    a. Cereal and coffee
    b. A backscratcher and a comb
    c. Lipstick and cigarettes
    d. Cigarettes and coffee cake

5. What does Ruth do for Beatrice while she tells her about Tillie?
    a. She tells her stories about the past.
    b. She combs her hair.
    c. She picks out all her clothes for the day.
    d. She scratches Beatrice's back with a backscratcher.

6. What is **the history** that Ruth refers to?
    a. The story of her family's lives kept by the school
    b. The story of the family's happy past
    c. The stories told in her American history class
    d. The story Beatrice tells about her father's wagon

Marigolds Multiple Choice Quizzes continued page 4

7. What is Ruth's favorite brand of cigarettes?
    a. L & M's
    b. Camels
    c. Kools
    d. Marlboros

Marigolds Multiple Choice Quizzes continued page 5

Section 3: From Tillie's second speech envisioning her science project to just prior to Nanny's entrance

1. In her vision, what does Tillie remember seeing behind the glass?
   a. She saw her mother dying.
   b. She saw her mother drinking whiskey.
   c. She saw a white cloud beginning to form.
   d. She saw her marigold seeds beginning to sprout.

2. What does Tillie say would happen to the fountain of smoke?
   a. It would go on for 15 minutes.
   b. It will be snuffed out in 10 minutes.
   c. It would go on for millions of years.
   d. It would slowly disappear from view.

3. When the lights come up, what is Tillie doing with her seeds?
   a. Tillie is planting her seeds.
   b. Tillie is feeding her seeds to the rabbit.
   c. Tillie is watching her seeds grow.
   d. Tillie is offering her seeds to her mother.

4. What kind of seeds are they?
   a. Asters
   b. Marigolds
   c. Pumpkin
   d. Sunflower

5. What have the seeds been exposed to?
   a. Cat urine
   b. Cobalt-60.
   c. Infrared lights
   d. Sunlight

6. What are two programs that Beatrice admits she never finished?
   a. The real estate course and beauty school
   b. Study for her GED and the college prep course
   c. A business course and an accounting review for starting her own business
   d. A nursing course and a special session on aging

7. What new business does Beatrice say she is thinking of going into?
   a. A bed and breakfast
   b. A hotel
   c. A tea shop.
   d. An old age home

Marigolds Multiple Choice Quizzes continued page 6

<u>Section 4: From Nanny's rustling at the curtains to the set's going dark after Beatrice talks about her "half-lifes"</u>

1. What is the first evidence seen of Nanny?
   a. Her big nose
   b. Her ugly feet
   c. Her cataracts
   d. Her thin and wrinkled hands.

2. What can be seen in Nanny's eyes?
   a. Total vacancy
   b. Great cataracts
   c. Lost love
   d. The past

3. What does Nanny's shuffling motion remind one of?
   a. Old man time
   b. A ticking clock
   c. The ocean
   d. Sad old times

4. How does Beatrice speak to Nanny?
   a. In a very kind way
   b. In an annoyed manner
   c. As though Nanny were her own mother
   d. As though the old woman were a deaf year-old child.

5. What is the difference between what Beatrice actually says to Nanny in capital letters and what she is thinking in lower case letters?
   a. In capital letters she talks loudly but kindly; in lower case letters she whispers sweet things.
   b. In capital letters she speaks nicely, but in lower case letters she says what she is really thinking.
   c. In capital letters she says things her daughters can hear; in lower case letters she says things she doesn't want them to know.
   d. In capital letters she speaks in English to Nanny, but in lower case letters she speaks Nanny's native Spanish.

6. What does Beatrice say Nanny's daughter is pretending to be?
   a. An important political leader
   b. Miss Career Woman of the Year
   c. Miss Know It All
   d. A fairy princess

Marigolds Multiple Choice Quizzes continued page 7

7. What one mistake does Beatrice say started her downfall?
   a. She failed her beauty school course.
   b. She didn't finish high school.
   c. She married the wrong man and got tied down with children.
   d. She had a second child.

8. What does Beatrice say she thinks she will do when Nanny's daughter comes to visit her mother again?
   a. Probably faint
   b. Yell at her
   c. Kick the woman
   d. Drop dead.

9. How does Beatrice say she is going to kill the rabbit?
   a. Chop its head off
   b. Chloroform it
   c. Feed it to the dog
   d. Put it out in the snow

10. What is Nanny's "duty"?
    a. To take financial care of her daughter
    b. To vote
    c. Telling the truth
    d. Going to the bathroom

Marigolds Multiple Choice Quizzes continued page 8

Section 5: From the sound of Beatrice's dialing the phone until she hangs up from talking with Mr. Goodman

1. Who is Beatrice trying to call on the phone?
   a. Her hairdresser
   b. The principal of her daughters' school
   c. Janice Vickery's mother
   d. Mr. Goodman.

2. What is Beatrice's last name?
   a. Carlton
   b. McMichael
   c. Gunther
   d. Hunsdorfer.

3. What job is Ruth doing for Mr. Goodman?
   a. She is babysitting his children.
   b. She is co-teaching a class with him.
   c. She is serving as a teacher's aide in his class.
   d. She is acting as Mr. Goodman's secretary.

4. What are three of Ruth's duties in her job with Mr. Goodman?
   a. Teaching, correcting papers, and disciplining the students
   b. Keeping attendance, taking care of the cut cards, and typing.
   c. Minding the children, feeding them lunch, and preparing Mr. Goodman's dinner
   d. Teaching two units of literature, making all writing assignments, and correcting all student papers

5. Why is Beatrice worried about Tillie's seeds?
   a. She thinks the rabbit will eat them.
   b. She thinks they will grow too big.
   c. She worries that they are stolen from the school.
   d. She worries about their being radioactive.

6. What two things is Beatrice doing while she talks with Mr. Goodman on the phone?
   a. Writing down everything he says and drawing pictures of him
   b. Yelling at Nanny and hugging Tillie
   c. Laughing and smoking a cigarette.
   d. Giggling and making funny faces at Tillie and Ruth

Marigolds Multiple Choice Quizzes continued page 9

Section 6: From the time that the music rises to thunder crashes until the stage goes dark after Beatrice tells Ruth about her nightmare

1. Who screams at the beginning of this section?
   a. The rabbit
   b. Ruth
   c. Beatrice
   d. Nanny

2. How does Beatrice divert Ruth's attention from her fright and make her laugh?
   a. She tells her an off-color joke.
   b. She lights a cigarette for her.
   c. She makes a comic face for her.
   d. She slaps her.

3. When the electricity goes off, what does Beatrice look for right away?
   a. A huge pink candle she has been keeping for that purpose
   b. A kerosene lamp
   c. A flashlight
   d. The little candles that were on her last year's birthday cake

4. What is the name of the man Ruth is supposedly so afraid of?
   a. Mr. Bogey Man
   b. Mr. Mayo
   c. Mr. Fields
   d. Joe Kelly

5. What story does Ruth want Beatrice to tell her?
   a. The story of the wagon
   b. Nice things about Ruth's father
   c. Old stories of how courageous Beatrice's father was during the war
   d. Stories about dead horses

6. What had Beatrice done with her father's wagon years ago?
   a. Burned it
   b. Ridden in it
   c. Gotten into it and driven it herself
   d. Steered it when her father got sick

7. What part of Beatrice's story doesn't Ruth want to hear?
   a. About the cat that dies
   b. The part about how Beatrice got married
   c. The part about Janice Vickery's winning science exhibit
   d. About the dead horses

Marigolds Multiple Choice Quizzes continued page 10

8. Where are Beatrice's parents now?
    a. They live in Florida.
    b. They moved to California just months ago.
    c. They are both living in nursing homes.
    d. They are both deceased.

9. Whose face does Beatrice see in the window in her own nightmare?
    a. Her dead father's
    b. A horse head
    c. Her mother smiling at her
    d. The man who sold her father fruit

Marigolds Multiple Choice Quizzes continued page 11

Section 7: From the time the lights come on Nanny at the kitchen table with the beer in front of her until the music starts and the lights fade after Tillie cries-END OF ACT I

1. Why does Beatrice say she hasn't killed the rabbit?
    a. Because Tillie would feel bad
    b. Because she can't figure out how to do it
    c. Because Ruth would have convulsions for fifty years as a result
    d. Because the rabbit is really kind of cute

2. What does Beatrice say she came up with when she took stock of her life?
    a. She came up with too much work to do by herself.
    b. She came up with a great plan to open a tea shop.
    c. She came up with "zero."
    d. She came up with a grand agenda.

3. What news does Ruth tell Beatrice about Tillie?
    a. That Tillie is pregnant
    b. That Tillie has been dating Chris Burns
    c. That Tillie is one of the finalists at a science fair
    d. That Tillie failed her science class

4. Who calls Beatrice on the phone and what does he want her to do?
    a. Mr. Goodman calls her and asks her to come to see him about Tillie.
    b. Dr. Berg, the principal, calls to invite her to sit on the stage with the other mothers at the science fair.
    c. Miss Hanley calls her to ask her to be nicer to Tillie.
    d. Mr. Goodman calls her to ask her to go out to dinner with him.

5. How does Beatrice react to Dr. Berg's invitation?
    a. She tells him she will definitely do it.
    b. She says no.
    c. She laughs out loud.
    d. She tells him she will think about it.

6. Who does Beatrice say she would look like up on the stage?
    a. Like Janice Vickery
    b. Like she used to when she was young
    c. Like Ruth when she was having a convulsion
    d. Like Tillie.

Marigolds Multiple Choice Quizzes continued page 12

7. What does Beatrice do when Tillie begins to cry?
   a. She embraces her.
   b. She yells at her to stop.
   c. She slaps her.
   d. She tells Ruth to make Tillie stop.

Marigolds Multiple Choice Quizzes continued page 13

Section 8: From the **BEGINNING OF ACT II** about two weeks later until Beatrice breaks into tears and decides not to go to the fair

1. What is Tillie preparing to do at the beginning of Act II?
   a. Preparing to water her seeds
   b. Preparing to run away from home
   c. Preparing to go out on a date
   d. Preparing to take her science project to the final judging of the science fair

2. What is the main title on the large screen that stands on one of the tables?
   a. WHY THE ATOM IS OUR FRIEND
   b. THE EFFECT OF GAMMA RAYS ON MAN-IN-THE-MOON MARIGOLDS
   c. ATOMIC THINGS ARE THE HOPE OF THE FUTURE
   d. WHY I SHOULD BE THE WINNER AT THE SCIENCE FAIR

3. What is the subtopic on the screen?
   a. MY SPECIAL PROJECT
   b. THE PAST; THE PRESENT; THE FUTURE.
   c. FASCINATING ATOMIC FACTS
   d. THINGS FROM LONG AGO AND NEWS OF THE FUTURE

4. Who does Ruth say is Tillie's only competition at the fair?
   a. Chris Burns
   b. Miss Hanley
   c. Janice Vickery.
   d. Herself

5. What item of Tillie's clothing does Ruth say will make people laugh?
   a. Her jumper
   b. Her hair bow
   c. Her shoes
   d. Her raggy slip

6. According to Ruth, how did Mr. Goodman say Beatrice sounded over the phone?
   a. Really nice and friendly
   b. Kind of frightened
   c. Drunk
   d. Crazy.

7. According to Ruth, what did Miss Hanley say Beatrice's nickname used to be?
   a. Betty Boop
   b. Bea the Weirdo
   c. Betty the Loon
   d. Loony tunes

Marigolds Multiple Choice Quizzes continued page 14

8. What did Janice Vickery boil in a pot?
   a. A lobster
   b. Some kale
   c. A cat
   d. A rabbit

9. Who is the boy that Ruth worries about being embarrassed in front of?
   a. Miss Hanley's nephew, Claude
   b. Chuck Goodman
   c. Janice Vickery's little brother
   d. Chris Burns.

10. Why does Tillie give her rabbit to Ruth?
    a. Because she knows that Ruth will take good care of it
    b. In exchange for some money to buy more marigold seeds
    c. Because she was tired of taking care of it herself
    d. In exchange for Ruth's agreeing not to tell Beatrice that people are laughing at her

11. What does Tillie say about Beatrice's appearance when Beatrice appears at the top of the stairs all dressed up?
    a. "Gosh, Mama, are you really going to wear that?"
    b. "Come on, Mama, we're really late!"
    c. "Mama, you look beautiful."
    d. "Good heavens, Mama, not the feather boa, please!"

12. What does Beatrice say happens to people who are just a little bit different in this world?
    a. People try to kill them off.
    b. People really like them.
    c. People give them awards.
    d. People wish they could be like them.

13. Why won't Beatrice let Ruth go along to school with her and Tillie?
    a. Because Ruth might have another seizure
    b. Because Ruth has been nasty to her
    c. Because Ruth only wants to go to jeer at Tillie
    d. Because someone has to stay home to care for Nanny

14. What does Beatrice say she feels in the back of her brain?
    a. Scared as heck
    b. Really upset at Tillie
    c. Kind of excited to be going out somewhere
    d. Just a little *proud*

Marigolds Multiple Choice Quizzes continued page 15

15. What does Ruth call Beatrice just as Beatrice starts to go out the door to get in the taxi?
    a. Mama, my beautiful Mama
    b. Pretty lady
    c. Betty the Loon
    d. You old biddy

Marigolds Multiple Choice Quizzes continued page 16

Section 9: From the beginning of Janice's presentation to the **END OF THE PLAY**

1. Where does Janice say she got the cat for her experiment?
   a. From the ASPCA
   b. From a nearby farm
   c. From Tillie
   d. From a child in her neighborhood

2. What does Janice say she boiled the cat in?
   a. Just plain salted water
   b. A sodium hydroxide solution
   c. Oil
   d. Oil and vinegar

3. What does Janice do between parts of her presentation?
   a. She sneers at the audience.
   b. She looks at her notes.
   c. She laughs.
   d. She looks for her friends in the audience.

4. What is Beatrice doing as the spotlight comes up on her?
   a. Dancing
   b. Drinking whiskey
   c. Going through a phone book
   d. Laughing with Nanny's daughter

5. What has Beatrice obviously been doing?
   a. Beatrice obviously has been working out.
   b. Beatrice obviously has been running.
   c. Beatrice obviously has been drinking.
   d. Beatrice obviously has been writing letters.

6. What message does Beatrice leave on the phone for Dr. Berg, Mr. Goodman, and Miss Hanley?
   a. She says to say thank them for making her wish she was dead.
   b. She says to tell them all to go to hell.
   c. She says for them to call her back right away.
   d. She says to say thanks for helping Tillie out.

7. Who does Beatrice call next?
   a. Miss Hanley's mother
   b. Nanny's daughter.
   c. The real estate course people
   d. The local college

Marigolds Multiple Choice Quizzes continued page 17

8. What does Beatrice tell Nanny's daughter?
   a. To stay away from Nanny
   b. To come and get Nanny by the next day.
   c. To visit her mother more often
   d. To write her mother some letters

9. What has Beatrice done to the rabbit while Tillie and Ruth were gone?
   a. She put it in a special cage.
   b. She killed it.
   c. She named it Peter.
   d. She gave it away to someone in the neighborhood.

10. Why doesn't Beatrice want to call the doctor when Ruth has another episode?
    a. Because the doctor has already come a hundred times
    b. Because the doctor never knows what to do
    c. Because she wants to keep her money for setting up a business.
    d. Because she doesn't have any cash in the house

11. What does Beatrice tell Tillie she hates?
    a. Both her and Ruth
    b. The world.
    c. Mr. Goodman
    d. Chris Burns

12. What does Tillie say is the most important thing her experiment has done?
    a. Tillie says her experiment has made her feel important.
    b. Tillie says her experiment has improved the whole world.
    c. Tillie says her experiment has made her mother happy.
    d. Tillie says her experiment has earned her an A+.

KEY: MULTIPLE CHOICE QUIZZES
The Effect of Gamma Rays on Man-in-the-Moon Marigolds

Section 1	Section 2	Section 3	Section 4
1 C	1 D	1 C	1 D
2 D	2 B	2 C	2 B
3 A	3 A	3 A	3 B
4 C	4 C	4 B	4 D
5 B	5 D	5 B	5 B
6 D	6 A	6 A	6 B
7 C	7 C	7 C	7 C
8 C			8 D
9 C			9 B
			10 D

Section 5	Section 6	Section 7	Section 8
1 D	1 B	1 C	1 D
2 D	2 C	2 C	2 B
3 D	3 D	3 C	3 B
4 B	4 B	4 B	4 C
5 D	5 A	5 D	5 B
6 C	6 C	6 D	6 D
	7 D	7 A	7 C
	8 D		8 C
	9 A		9 D
			10 D
			11 C
			12 A
			13 D
			14 D
			15 C

Section 9
1 A
2 B
3 C
4 C
5 C
6 A
7 B
8 B
9 B
10 C
11 B
12 A

PRE-READING VOCABULARY WORKSHEETS

VOCABULARY
The Effects of Gamma Rays on Man-in-the-Moon Marigolds

Section 1 Part I: Using Prior Knowledge and Contextual Clues
Below are the sentences in which the vocabulary words appear in the text. Read the sentence. Use any clues you can find in the sentence combined with your prior knowledge, and write what you think the underlined words mean in the space provided.

1. The lights go down slowly as music creeps in-a theme for lost children, the near **misbegotten**.

2. Or perhaps this part of me became lost in a terrible beast, or became part of a huge bird that flew above the **primeval** swamps.

3. And he called this bit of me an **atom**.

4. I never saw a man with a more **effeminate** face in my life.

5. The idea of letting her teach girl's gym is **staggering**.

6. Any daughter that would turn her mother in as the administrator of a concentration camp has got to be suffering from something very **peculiar**.

7 On **radioactivity**-

8. If we wait a minute longer this house is going to **ferment**.

9. Do you want me to **chloroform** that thing right this minute?

Part II: Determining the Meaning
Match the vocabulary words to their dictionary definitions.

___ 1. misbegotten   A. to anesthetize or kill with chloroform
___ 2. ferment   B. spontaneous emission of radiation
___ 3. effeminate   C. to seethe; to be agitated
___ 4. primeval   D. of dubious origins
___ 5. staggering   E. having qualities usually associated with females
___ 6. atom   F. belonging to the first or earliest age or ages
___ 7. peculiar   G. smallest unit of an element
___ 8. radioactivity   H. odd
___ 9. chloroform   I. overwhelming

Marigolds Vocabulary continued page 2

Section 2 Part I: Using Prior Knowledge and Contextual Clues
Below are the sentences in which the vocabulary words appear in the text. Read the sentence. Use any clues you can find in the sentence combined with your prior knowledge, and write what you think the underlined words mean in the space provided.

1. You're **exaggerating**…

2. And there was Tillie, cranking away, looking weird as a **coot**…

3. Matilda turned me in to the **Gestapo**.

4. Using the backscratcher on Beatrice, who squirms with **ecstasy**.

5. **Psoriasis**?

Part II: Determining the Meaning
Match the vocabulary words to their dictionary definitions.

___ 1. exaggerating   A. a skin disease
___ 2. coot   B. intense joy or delight
___ 3. Gestapo   C. enlarging, increasing beyond normal bounds
___ 4. ecstasy   D. an eccentric person
___ 5. psoriasis   E. German security police during Nazi regime

Marigolds Vocabulary continued page 3

Section 3 Part I: Using Prior Knowledge and Contextual Clues
Below are the sentences in which the vocabulary words appear in the text. Read the sentence. Use any clues you can find in the sentence combined with your prior knowledge, and write what you think the underlined words mean in the space provided.

1. Atoms exploding, **flinging** off tiny bullets that caused the fountain, atom after atom breaking down into something new.

2. It would go on for millions of years-on and on, this fountain from **eternity**.

3. If there's one thing I've always wanted, it's been a living room planted with **marigolds** that have been exposed to cobalt-60.

4. Just let me keep them here for a week or so until they get started and then I'll **transplant** them to the backyard.

5. She **calculates**.

Part II: Determining the Meaning
Match the vocabulary words to their dictionary definitions.

___ 1. flinging   A. computes mathematically
___ 2. eternity   B. American plant with yellow or orange flowers
___ 3. marigolds   C. uproot and replant
___ 4. transplant   D. casting aside; discarding
___ 5. calculates   E. continuance without beginning or end

Marigolds Vocabulary continued page 4

Section 4 Part I: Using Prior Knowledge and Contextual Clues
Below are the sentences in which the vocabulary words appear in the text. Read the sentence. Use any clues you can find in the sentence combined with your prior knowledge, and write what you think the underlined words mean in the space provided.

1. There is a **rustling** at the curtains.

2. Two thin and wrinkled hands push the curtains apart slowly and then the **ancient** face of Nanny appears.

3. If one looked closely, great **cataracts** could be seen on each eye, and it is certain that all that can pierce her soundless prison are mere shadows from the outside world.

4. She **pervades** the room with age.

5. What does **half-life** mean?

6. **Reciting** from memory.

7. Then, in a loud, horribly **saccharine** voice, she speaks to Nanny as if she were addressing a deaf year-old child.

8. Nanny has seated herself at a table, smiling but **oblivious** to her environment.

9. There is a pause as the woman's **shuffling** continues.

10. The lights go low on Tillie, Nanny becomes a **silhouette**, and the light remains on Beatrice.

Part II: Determining the Meaning
Match the vocabulary words to their dictionary definitions.

___ 1. rustling
___ 2. ancient
___ 3. cataracts
___ 4. pervades
___ 5. half-life
___ 6. reciting
___ 7. saccharine
___ 8. oblivious
___ 9. shuffling
___ 10. silhouette

A. repeating or uttering aloud
B. sweet
C. outline or profile
D. soft fluttering or crackling sounds
E. very old
F. opacities of the eye lens or capsule
G. spreads throughout
H. sliding feet along the floor
I. unaware of
J. time for half of nuclei to radioactively decay

Marigolds Vocabulary continued page 5

Section 5 Part I: Using Prior Knowledge and Contextual Clues
Below are the sentences in which the vocabulary words appear in the text. Read the sentence. Use any clues you can find in the sentence combined with your prior knowledge, and write what you think the underlined words mean in the space provided.

1. You were paying so much attention to Matilda that I'll bet Ruth got **jealous**.

2. She's a terrible **snoop**…

3. Now, she told me they had been subjected to radioactivity, and I hear such terrible things about radioactivity that I automatically associate radioactivity with **sterility**…

4. …and it positively **horrifies** me to have those seeds right here in my living room.

5. No, I must admit that at this very moment I don't know what a **mutation** is…

Part II: Determining the Meaning
Match the vocabulary words to their dictionary definitions.

___ 1. jealous   A. a change, as in nature, form, or quality
___ 2. snoop   B. envious
___ 3. sterility   C. scares; shocks; causes horror
___ 4. horrifies   D. one who pries secretly
___ 5. mutation   E. incapability of producing offspring

Marigolds Vocabulary continued page 6

Section 6 Part I: Using Prior Knowledge and Contextual Clues
Below are the sentences in which the vocabulary words appear in the text. Read the sentence. Use any clues you can find in the sentence combined with your prior knowledge, and write what you think the underlined words mean in the space provided.

1. The music theme comes in, in a minor key, softly at first, but **accentuated** by increasingly loud pulses which transmute into thunder crashes.

2. Ruth appears on the landing and releases another scream which breaks off into **gasps**.

3. There is another tremendous thunder crash as Beatrice comes out of her room, puts on the hall light, and catches the **hysterical** girl on the stairs.

4. That big bad **bogey man**?

5. She **rummage** through one of the boxes and grabs a blanket.

6. I had more **nerve** than a bear when I was a kid.

7. And then Papa got sick…and I drove with him up to the **sanatorium**.

8. I never had nightmares over the fights with your father, or the divorce, or his **thrombosis**-he deserved it-I never had nightmares over any of that.

Part II: Determining the Meaning
Match the vocabulary words to their dictionary definitions.

___ 1. accentuated   A. blood clot in blood vessel or heart
___ 2. gasps   B. makes a disorderly search of
___ 3. hysterical   C. a terrifying presence; hobgoblin
___ 4. bogey man   D. stressed; accented
___ 5. rummages   E. brazen boldness
___ 6. nerve   F. a place of convalescence from illness
___ 7. sanatorium   G. sharp breaths
___ 8. thrombosis   H. having excessive or uncontrollable emotion

Marigolds Vocabulary continued page 7

Section 7 Part I: Using Prior Knowledge and Contextual Clues
Below are the sentences in which the vocabulary words appear in the text. Read the sentence. Use any clues you can find in the sentence combined with your prior knowledge, and write what you think the underlined words mean in the space provided.

1. Tillie comes in the front door with a box of large marigold plants and sets them down where they'll be **inconspicuous**.

2. You can start by getting rid of that rabbit or I'll **suffocate** the bastard.

3. I'd chloroform the thing myself, but that crazy sister of yours would throw **convulsions** for fifty years…

4. …and I hate a house that **vibrates**.

5. …and Mr. Goodman told me himself during the eighth period in the office when I was **eavesdropping**

6. A chord of finality **punctuates** the end of Act I.

Part II: Determining the Meaning
Match the vocabulary words to their dictionary definitions.

___ 1. inconspicuous   A. emphasizes
___ 2. suffocate   B. not readily noticeable
___ 3. convulsions   C. shakes or trembles
___ 4. vibrates   D. listening secretly
___ 5. eavesdropping   E. kill by preventing access to oxygen
___ 6. punctuates   F. intense involuntary muscular contractions

Marigolds Vocabulary continued page 8

Section 8 Part I: Using Prior Knowledge and Contextual Clues
Below are the sentences in which the vocabulary words appear in the text. Read the sentence. Use any clues you can find in the sentence combined with your prior knowledge, and write what you think the underlined words mean in the space provided.

1. She almost appears to be **sinister**.

2. The only **competition** you have to worry about is Janice Vickery.

3. Betty the **Loon**…

4. If you ask me, they should've sent all the parents a **mimeographed** sheet of   instructions.

5. …and the only thing I'd have to say is, what a pack of stupid teachers and **vicious** children they have.

6. …do you know, sometimes you **exasperate** me?

7. Almost **berserk**.

8. Beatrice breaks into tears that shudder her body, and the lights go down slowly on her **pathetic** form.

Part II: Determining the Meaning
Match the vocabulary words to their dictionary definitions.

    ___ 1. sinister   A. arousing sympathy and compassion
    ___ 2. competition   B. copied
    ___ 3. loon   C. deranged; crazed
    ___ 4. mimeographed   D. make angry or impatient
    ___ 5. vicious   E. threatening evil
    ___ 6. exasperate   F. savage; evil; dangerous
    ___ 7. berserk   G. one who is crazy or simple-minded
    ___ 8. pathetic   H. other competitors capable of winning

Marigolds Vocabulary continued page 9

Section 9 Part I: Using Prior Knowledge and Contextual Clues
Below are the sentences in which the vocabulary words appear in the text. Read the sentence. Use any clues you can find in the sentence combined with your prior knowledge, and write what you think the underlined words mean in the space provided.

1. Her face and voice are **smug**.

2. I mean, as it is now, it's extremely useful for students of **anatomy**, even with the missing rib bones…

3. That finished, she turns and **surveys** the room again.

4. The ringing **triggers** off something else she wants to do.

5. The seeds were exposed to various degrees…of **gamma rays** from radiation sources in Oak Ridge…

6. Beatrice continues **mechanically** on down the stairs.

7. Beatrice **commences** tacking up one of the curtains.

8. Ruth commences to **tremble**.

Part II: Determining the Meaning
Match the vocabulary words to their dictionary definitions.

___ 1. smug
___ 2. anatomy
___ 3. surveys
___ 4. triggers
___ 5. gamma rays
___ 6. mechanically
___ 7. commences
___ 8. tremble

A. starts
B. precipitates; causes to happen
C. examines; looks at comprehensively
D. self-satisfied; complacent
E. like a machine
F. structure of an organism or organ
G. electromagnetic radiation
H. shake violently

53

ANSWER KEY - VOCABULARY
The Effect of Gamma Rays on Man-in-the-Moon Marigolds

Section 1	Section 2	Section 3	Section 4	Section 5
1 D	1 C	1 D	1 D	1 B
2 C	2 D	2 E	2 E	2 D
3 E	3 E	3 B	3 F	3 E
4 F	4 B	4 C	4 G	4 C
5 I	5 A	5 A	5 J	5 A
6 G			6 A	
7 H			7 B	
8 B			8 I	
9 A			9 H	
			10 C	

Section 6	Section 7	Section 8	Section 9
1 D	1 B	1 E	1 D
2 G	2 E	2 H	2 F
3 H	3 F	3 G	3 C
4 C	4 C	4 B	4 B
5 B	5 D	5 F	5 G
6 E	6 A	6 D	6 E
7 F		7 C	7 A
8 A		8 A	8 H

DAILY LESSONS

Lesson One

Objectives
1. To introduce the unit on **The Effect of Gamma Rays on Man-in-the-Moon Marigolds**
2. To distribute books and other related materials
3. To read "Marigolds Revisited" by Paul Zindel
4. To begin consideration and discussion of one theme in **Marigolds**, namely having a dream

NOTE: Prior to this lesson, students should have been assigned to bring in some physical item (or a written physical description, photograph, or drawing of that item) that symbolizes their special dream. Borrowing from the story line in **Marigolds** in which Beatrice and Tillie both have a special dream, students should be encouraged to think about what dreams they would like to realize in their lifetime. You will have prepared ahead of time a bulletin board that has the title MY DREAM: THE THING I MOST WANT TO ACHIEVE. You may want to place pictures on the board. Remember to include pictures of both tangible and intangible things. For instance, you might have some valuable possessions pictured but will also want to show pictures of people embracing, people laughing together, people talking with doctors, etc. The point, of course, is that our most cherished dreams may be to achieve good health, to reach a deeper spiritual relationship, and to gain new friendships and strengthen old ones as to achieve a more tangible goal.

Activity #1
Ask students individually to explain the significance to them of their special dreams. If they can, they might explain how long they have had the dream, how they came to have it, what they think are their chances of achieving it, and when they think they might achieve it. After they have explained this, each student should go to the bulletin board and write a few words (using the infinitive "to") to describe their most cherished dream. If they have a picture representing their dream and there is space on the bulletin board, the students might post their pictures on the board as well. Students should be encouraged to keep all valuables with them and not leave them lying around in the classroom.

Activity #2
Distribute the materials students will use in this unit. Explain in details how students are to use the materials.

Lesson One continued page 2

Study Guides Students should read the study guide questions for each reading assignment before beginning the assignment to get a feeling for what events and ideas are important in the section they are about to read. After reading the section, students will (as a class or individually) answer the questions to review the important events and ideas from that section of the book. Students should keep the study guides as study materials for the unit test.

Vocabulary As they are reading a section of the text, students will do vocabulary work related to the section they are reading. If they hunt for the vocabulary words as they read, students should be able to figure out the contextual meaning of the words. Following the completion of the reading of the book, there will be a vocabulary review of all the words used in the vocabulary assignments. Students should keep their vocabulary work as study materials for the unit test. A special note: The words in this play are generally not very difficult. For some sections of the text, students will have little trouble matching up words with definitions. If you wish to make the vocabulary unit more challenging for your students, you might try having them use the words in sentences **not** relating to **Marigolds** and possibly trying to use all of the words in one section in a paragraph.

Reading Assignment Sheet You need to fill in the reading assignment sheet to let students know when their reading has to be completed. You can either write the assignment on a side black board or bulletin board and leave it there for students to see each day, or you can make copies for each student to have. In any case, advise students to become very familiar with the reading assignments so they know what is expected of them.

Extra Activities Center The Extra Activities portion of this unit contains suggestions for a library of related books and articles in your classroom as well as crossword and word search puzzles. Make a center in your room where you will keep these materials for students to use. (Bring the books and articles in from the library and keep several copies of the puzzles on hand.) Explain to students that these materials are available for their use when they finish reading assignments or other class work early.

Nonfiction Assignment Sheet Explain to students that they each are to read at least one nonfiction piece from the in-class library at some time during the unit. Students will fill out a nonfiction assignment sheet after completing the reading to help you evaluate their reading experiences and to help the students to think about and evaluate their own reading.

Books Each school has its own rules and regulations regarding student use of school books. Advise students of the procedures that are usual for your school.

Activity #2
The very short essay, "Marigolds Revisited" by Paul Zindel is in copies of **Marigolds**. If you cannot find it in one text, you surely will find it in another and can copy it for your students to read. Because so much of Zindel's writing is autobiographical, it will be important to your students' understanding of the play to have them read what Zindel wrote about it twenty-five years after it was first published.

NONFICTION ASSIGNMENT SHEET
(To be completed after reading the required nonfiction article)

Name _____ Date _____ Class _____

Title of Nonfiction Read _____

Author _____ Publication Date _____

I. **Factual Summary**: Write a short summary of the piece you read.

II. **Vocabulary**:
1. Which vocabulary words were difficult?

2. What did you do to help yourself understand the words?

III. **Interpretation**: What was the main point the author wanted you to get from reading his or her work?

IV. **Criticism**:
1. Which points of the piece did you agree with or find easy to believe? Why?

2. Which points did you disagree with or find hard to believe? Why?

V. **Personal Response**:
1. What do you think about this piece?

2. How does this piece help you better understand the play, **The Effect of Gamma Rays on Man-in-the-Moon Marigolds**?

ORAL READING EVALUATION
The Effect of Gamma Rays on Man-in-the-Moon Marigolds

Name _____ Class _____ Date _____

SKILL	EXCELLENT	GOOD	AVERAGE	FAIR	POOR
Fluency	5	4	3	2	1
Clarity	5	4	3	2	1
Audibility	5	4	3	2	1
Pronunciation	5	4	3	2	1
_____	5	4	3	2	1
_____	5	4	3	2	1

Total _____ Grade _____

Comments:

Lesson Two

Objectives
1. To preview with study questions, do the vocabulary on, and read Section 1.
2. To give students practice reading orally
3. To evaluate students' oral reading
4. To allow students to do Section 2 preview work at home

Activity #1
Have students read Section 1 out loud in class. You probably know the best way to choose readers from your class: pick students at random, ask for volunteers, or use whatever other method works best for your group. If you have not yet completed an oral reading evaluation for your students this marking period, this would be a good opportunity to do so. A form is included with this unit for your convenience.

If students do not complete reading through Section 1 in class, they should do so prior to your next class meeting.

Activity #2
Ask students to do the preview work for Section 2

Lesson Three

Objectives
1. To review the main events and ideas from Section 1
2. To read Section 2

Activity #1
Spend a short time reviewing Section 1 to make sure that students are reading carefully. Tell students that because the sections of text assigned are so short, they can read and then re-read them to gain thorough understanding.

Activity #2
Have students read Section 2, either silently or out loud in class. With a play such as this one, it might be helpful to have one student read a line or dialogue and then ask another student how he or she would read the line. If time permits, have three or four students read the same line out loud to demonstrate how differently it could be delivered on stage. Extra time spent now will pay off later in the play.

Lesson Four

Objectives
1. To review Section 2
2. To do the pre-reading and reading for Section 3
3. To introduce the Nonfiction Reading Assignment (which follows)

Activity #1
Review the second section of the text. Because sections are relatively short, your reviews may be short as well. The purpose of the reviews is just to see that the students are keeping up and are understanding the nuances of the text.

Activity #2
Give students a few minutes to formulate answers for the study guide questions for Section 3 and then discuss the answers to the questions in detail. Each time you review the main events and ideas in a section of the book, you can use the short answer questions to guide the discussion, if you like. Then use the multiple choice quizzes when suggested in the unit guidelines or at any time that you think they will be useful to the students. For the short answers, write them on the board or overhead transparency so students can have the correct answers for study purposes.

Note: It is a good practice in public speaking and leadership skills for individual students to take charge of leading the discussions of the study questions. Perhaps a different student could go to the front of the class and lead the discussion each day that the study questions are discussed during this unit. You will still guide the discussion when appropriate and be sure to fill in any gaps the students leave.

Activity #3
Get students started on the Nonfiction Reading Assignment. Spend some time making sure they understand how to use the NFRA form that you have already handed out.

NONFICTION READING ASSIGNMENT

One of the dreams that Beatrice has in **The Effect of Gamma Rays on Man-in-the-Moon Marigolds** is to start her own business and to make money at it. Although starting one's own business is difficult, there are many resources available today for the person who wants to do so.

For this assignment, you are to read about starting a new business. After you have finished your reading, you should complete the Nonfiction Assignment Sheet that your teacher has already handed out. Also, be prepared to do a brief report in class about what you have learned in your research.

If you think it might be helpful to you, you can use the KWL form that follows both to steer your research and to keep your thoughts organized for an oral classroom report.

Topics for Nonfiction Reading Assignment:

Someone who started his or her own business and was successful
Good fields to go into today
The difference between working at a specific location and working from home
The special difficulties of working at home
Starting a business over the internet
Advertising concerns
Financial concerns
Should a business be incorporated?
How long does it take to make a profit?
Is it a good idea to go into business with a partner?
How does one choose a name for the business?
Big businesses that were once a small dream

If you want to write on a different topic, you need to speak to your teacher. If you do that, you should have a specific topic in mind that you wish to substitute for one of the above. But you may use a different topic only if your teacher agrees.

KWL
Marigolds

Directions: Before reading, think about what you already know about your assigned topic. Write the information in the K column. Think about what you would like to find out from reading the book. Write your questions in the W column. After you have read the book, use the L column to write the answers to your questions from the W column and anything else you remember from the book.

K (What I Know)	W (What I Want to Find Out)	L (What I Learned)

Lesson Five

Objectives
1.   To review Section 3
2.   To give students the opportunity to write to inform

Activity #1
Spend some time reviewing the third section of the text. Make sure that students are keeping up with the reading. Because the sections are short, students may think that it is okay to put their reading off until they start to fall behind. Encourage them, instead, to read and then to re-read so that they gain a full understanding of the characters, plots, and themes of the play.

Activity #2
Give students time to do Writing Assignment #1 (Writing to Inform) in class. An assignment sheet follows.

WRITING ASSIGNMENT #1
The Effect of Gamma Rays on Man-in-the-Moon Marigolds

PROMPT
In **The Effect of Gamma Rays on Man-in-the-Moon Marigolds**, Beatrice talks about going into business and making money. Although going into business for oneself can be enjoyable and rewarding, it is also difficult. It takes time, energy, and at least some money. You have already done some reading about starting a business when you did the Nonfiction Reading Assignment. Now use that information to write to inform.

Your assignment is to address someone who would like to start his or her own business. Assume that the person has asked you a question that relates to the study you did for the Nonfiction Reading Assignment. Formulate a specific question that the person might ask: the question should start HOW DO I…? Your assignment will be to write a paper to answer the person's question. That is writing to inform. Be sure that your question is a "How to" one so that you do not slip over into writing to give advice or to persuade. Your assignment is to write a composition in which you explain how to do what your audience wants to know about.

PRE-WRITING
Think through how you will answer your audience's question. Make a list of things that would have to be done. Try then to combine those items into categories. Having three categories of things (or just three things) would make writing the assignment easy and would keep you organized.

DRAFTING
Write an introductory paragraph in which you tell what you are writing about and state the question you will be answering. Try to make the first paragraph interesting enough so that people will want to read further. You might mention the three categories of things or things that you will discuss. In the body of the composition, explain how to do each of the three things. Be sure to tell all of the steps necessary and not simply assume that your audience will know what to do. And, finally, write a concluding paragraph in which you explain what has been explained in the rest of the paper. As with the first paragraph, try to make your conclusion as interesting as possible.

PROMPT
When you finish the rough draft of your paper, ask a student who sits near you to read it. After reading your draft, he or she should tell you what he or she liked best about your work, which parts were difficult to understand, and ways in which your work could be improved. Reread your paper considering your critic's comments, and make the corrections you think are necessary.

PROOFREADING
Do a final proofreading of your paper, double checking your grammar, spelling, organization, and the clarity of your ideas.

Lesson Six

Objectives
1. To do the pre-reading and reading for Section 4
2. To give students the opportunity to think about the characters in **Marigolds**

Activity #1
Spend a little time doing the pre-reading activities for the fourth section of the text. Because the section is short, you should need to allot just a brief period of time for this activity.

Activity #2
Break students into small groups and have them read Section 4 silently in their group.

Activity #3
Keep students in the small groups for the third activity. Assign each group one of these characters: Beatrice, Tillie, Ruth, Nanny, or Mr. Goodman. Ask students to think about their assigned character and then tell what they would like most and least about being that character and what they think that character most wants out of their life. After students have had some time to work on this activity, have them report their decisions to the rest of the class. Don't worry if there is some overlap and more than one section is assigned to a single character. That will make the reporting even more interesting.

Lesson Seven

Objective
    To give students the opportunity to think about going into business for themselves

Activity
One of the best things about literature is that it often encourages us to think about our own lives and to look at the choices we are making. Today more and more people are deciding to leave their places of employment in favor of starting their own businesses.

This class project--Project New Business--will encourage students to think about their work lives and will possibly give them some tools for making decisions about the kinds of work they will do.

Directions for the project follow.

PROJECT NEW BUSINESS
The Effect of Gamma Rays on Man-in-the-Moon Marigolds

Objectives
Project Animal Rescue is a total class project for use in conjunction with the play, **The Effects of Gamma Rays on Man-in-the-Moon Marigolds** by Paul Zindel. Since one of the main ideas in the book deals with Beatrice's dream of starting her own business, this is a good opportunity to acquaint students with how people start businesses of their own. Doing this is difficult, but it can also be very rewarding, personally, professionally, and financially. This project is a way to make your students aware of the problems and the rewards of starting a new business and the growing movement in this country toward people's attempting to start their own businesses or at least to make arrangements to work out of their own homes.

Most communities have a branch of the Small Business Association in their communities. You can use that organization as part of this project. Doing this will require that you make a few phone inquiries ahead of time to be sure that necessary resources are available to your students. If there is no SBA in your area, then try contacting the owner of a small, relatively new business who would be willing to work with your class.

THE PROJECT
This project is separate from the rest of the **Marigolds** unit, so you can either use it while you are reading and reviewing the play or as a separate mini-unit after you have completed the unit test for **Marigolds**. Also, having it as a separate project enables you to either eliminate it or to use it, without disturbing the flow of the unit as a whole.

Assignment #1
Your community should have either a branch of the Small Business Association or perhaps a local entrepreneur available to talk with your class. Find several reports/articles on business owners in your region, or your state, and show them to your students. Use them as a springboard for a discussion of the problem of starting a new business. (Note: Sometimes even very small community newspapers and newsletters will present this kind of information. If not, try calling the owner of your community newspaper to get the name of someone who has started his or her own business in the area.)

Assignment #2
As a class, write a letter requesting either someone from the SBA or a local business owner to come to your class to discuss the problems, challenges, and rewards of going into business for oneself. Send the letter and then make any necessary follow-up phone calls to make arrangements for the visit.

Assignment #3
After students have the information you gather on the new businesses, send them to the library to do some research. This research should fit nicely with the preliminary investigation that students did for their Nonfiction Reading Assignment and wrote about in Writing Assignment $#1. Each student should be able to read and summarize at least two articles on the topic. Hint: Refer

students back to the list of topics for the NFRA. However, if they have become interested in some other topic, you might allow them to investigate something other than the topic that they did for the NFRA and Writing Assignment #1. If time allows in your class, this might even be a good time to have students choose a type of business that they would like to set up and follow through with the steps necessary to actually establish the business.

Assignment #4
After students have done their research, have them give oral reports about the articles they have read so that all students are exposed to the wealth of information that has been collectively read.

Assignment #5
Host the person who was invited to class in Assignment #2. This assignment should be done prior to undertaking Assignment #6.

Assignment #6
Divide students into groups of five or six. Explain that their job is to make a list of problems people might encounter in starting their own business and to brainstorm ways that those problems could be solved and the people could go on to create and run successful business operations.

Students might focus, for example, on the need that people face to get enough money together to go into business for themselves. Students could investigate various loans and grants available to new small business owners. Or they might want to look at ways to start a new business over the internet so that the new owner would need relatively little capital to get started.

Appropriate class time will need to be spent on this brainstorming. After the brainstorming has been done, have each student focus on one way that he or she can state and resolve one challenge faced by someone who wants to start a new business. The way that each students chooses should involve some amount of human interaction (letter writing, advertising discussion groups, writing an article for the newspaper, having speakers talk at all local schools and/or community centers, other educational campaigns, etc.)

Assignment #8
Have students follow through on their ideas for ways to eliminate the challenges of starting a new business. If they have chosen letter writing, for example, have them actually write helpful letters to the editor. If they think that an educational program would be useful to prospective business owners, have them design the program.

Project continued page 3

You might want to use some class time to allow students to update the rest of the class on what steps they are taking. Sometimes the other students may be able to make suggestions and criticisms that will be helpful in carrying out the project.

Assignment #9
After the project is finished, have a short wrap-up to allow students to discuss the value of what they have learned.

Lesson Eight

Objectives
1. To review Section 4
2. To do the pre-reading and reading for Section 5
3. To allow students to give updates on their Nonfiction Reading Assignments and/or their projects **or**
4. To give students some experience in role playing

Activity #1
Spend a few minutes reviewing the fourth section of the play to be sure that students are doing the reading and are understanding the play.

Activity #2
Take some time to do the pre-reading activities for Section 5. Give students time to read-either silently or out loud-the very short fifth section of the text.

Activity #3
Allow students a brief period to give updates on their Nonfiction Reading Assignments and/or their class projects, or

Activity #4
Spend some time with Beatrice's phone conversation with Mr. Goodman and allow students to role play. Give several students the opportunity to "play" Beatrice by breaking her conversation into parts (possibly before she lights her cigarette and after each of her puffs on the cigarette) and having different students read the parts out loud. You might want to start the exercise by choosing a student who will be comfortable reading out loud and playing part. When the whole conversation has been read, simply start all over again, or, if you like, let students fill in what they think Mr. Goodman's parts of the conversation would be if he spoke during it.

Lesson Nine

Objective
To give students the opportunity to write from personal experience

Activity
Have students do Writing Assignment #2 (Writing from Personal Experience). Directions for the assignment follow.

WRITING ASSIGNMENT #2
The Effects of Gamma Rays on Man-in-the-Moon Marigolds

PROMPT

In **The Effects of Gamma Rays on Man-in-the-Moon Marigolds**, the characters have unrealized dreams. Beatrice wants her own business. Tillie would like to go into science and to be herself. Everybody has a dream that they would like to realize. Some of us want to travel. Others hope to become a member of some particular profession. Still others want to make lots of money. And some people want to achieve less tangible dreams, such as living to see the world at peace or making a lifelong friendship.

Your assignment is to write about your most important dream. Assume that you are going to tell where the dream came from, what steps you have taken to achieve the dream, what you think your chances are of reaching it, how you expect to reach it, and/or what the effects of realizing the dream will be on your life and possibly the lives of others. Although the impetus to write about dreams came from **Marigolds**, you needn't write anything about the play for this assignment. This paper is about **your** personal dream.

PRE-WRITING

Think about how you want to explain your dream to your audience and how you would like to answer some of the questions posed above. Jot down some ideas about your dream. Then figure out a logical way to present your ideas. You might, for example, want to tell the dream's history, what you have done in the past to realize the dream, and what you plan to do in the future to realize it.

DRAFTING

Write an introductory paragraph in which you explain your dream. Try to make the first paragraph interesting enough so that people will want to read further. In the body of the composition, answer the question or questions you have chosen. If, for example, you have chosen to answer only one question, try to break the answer into parts and place one part in each of your paragraphs. Keep your audience in mind at all times. Make sure that you're not simply indulging yourself but that you are presenting information in a way that a reader would appreciate. And, finally, write a concluding paragraph in which you summarize or point to a future development or end with a question, or do whatever you think will leave the reader interested in your topic.

PROMPT

When you finish the rough draft of your paper, ask a student who sits near you to read it. After reading your draft, he or she should tell you what he or she liked best about your work, which parts were difficult to understand, and ways in which your work could be improved. Reread your paper considering your critic's comments, and make the corrections you think are necessary.

PROOFREADING

Do a final proofreading of your paper, double checking your grammar, spelling, organization, and the clarity of your ideas.

Lesson Ten

Objectives
1. To review Section 5
2. To do the pre-reading and reading for Section 6

Activity #1
Spend some time reviewing the fifth section of the book. Because it has already been read and perhaps even acted out in class, you should need relatively little time for review.

Activity #2
Give students time to do the pre-reading activities and the reading for Section 6. If you have not already evaluated students' oral reading abilities, this might be a good time to do so using the Oral Reading Evaluation form presented earlier.

Lesson Eleven

Objectives
1. To review Section 6
2. To do the pre-reading and reading for Section 7
3. To give students the opportunity to write to persuade

Activity #1
Give students a little time to review Section 6. If you like, you might spend a little time discussing the way that readers might respond differently to Beatrice after hearing her wagon story and hearing about her nightmare. One of the many interesting things about **Marigolds** is the way readers' opinions of the characters change as the play progresses and as we learn more and more about the characters and their personal motivations.

Activity #2
Spend a little class time doing the pre-reading activities and reading for Section 7.

Activity #3
Get students started on Writing Assignment #3 (Writing to Persuade). Directions follow.

WRITING ASSIGNMENT #3
The Effects of Gamma Rays on Man-in-the-Moon Marigolds

PROMPT
In **The Effects of Gamma Rays on Man-in-the-Moon Marigolds**, the characters are very different and very interesting. Different readers have different views of the people in the play. Some readers will like one character while other readers will dislike that character and like others. These differences are one of the things that make literature so interesting and informative.

Your assignment is to choose your favorite character to this point in the play and to write about why you think that character is the best. First, you will naturally have to define what makes a character "the best." Maybe you think the character would make the best friend, or maybe you think that the character is the smartest, or the funniest, or the most courageous. It doesn't matter how you define "the best" character, only that you explain your definition clearly to your audience. This paper is to persuade your audience that you have made a good choice. If possible, you should get your audience to agree with, or at least respect the reasoning behind, your choice.

PRE-WRITING
Think about why you have chosen your character. What makes the character interesting to you? Then jot down some examples that support your point of view. If you think the character is the most courageous, then jot down examples of the character acting courageously. Then figure out a logical way to present your ideas. You might, for example, want to explain your criteria, then show three separate examples of how the character meets that criteria. And finally, in a concluding paragraph, you might explain what you have already done in the body of the composition and try to leave the reader with some interesting idea or question to pursue.

DRAFTING
Write an introductory paragraph in which you tell what you explain your dream. Try to make the first paragraph interesting enough so that people will want to read further. In the body of the composition, answer the question or questions you have chosen. If, for example, you have chosen to answer only one question, try to break the answer into parts and place one part in each of your paragraphs. Keep your audience in mind at all times. Make sure that you're not simply indulging yourself but that you are presenting information in a way that a reader would appreciate. And, finally, write a concluding paragraph in which you summarize or point to a future development or end with a question, or do whatever you think will leave the reader interested in your topic.

PROMPT
When you finish the rough draft of your paper, ask a student who sits near you to read it. After reading your draft, he or she should tell you what he or she liked best about your work, which parts were difficult to understand, and ways in which your work could be improved. Reread your paper considering your critic's comments, and make the corrections you think are necessary.

PROOFREADING
Do a final proofreading of your paper, double checking your grammar, spelling, organization, and the clarity of your ideas.

Lesson Twelve

Objective
To give students an opportunity to understand the characters in **Marigolds** better by envisioning them in different contexts

Activity
Try to put aside one entire class to achieve this objective. What you are going to do is ask some of your students to do some role playing in front of the rest of the class. Because not everyone will have the opportunity to play a role in class, the other students will learn from observing. Both actors and observers should be encouraged to think about how the characters are going to act in each scenario. You will be the best judge of which students can be relied on to carry out the assignment with a reasonable degree of understanding and comfort.

Don't worry that you don't have enough time to accommodate this kind of role playing. Its object is not to rehearse or spend a lot of time preparing for the role playing. It is, instead, to think through very quickly how a character will act based on what students already know about them.

This activity will work best if you try to prepare the students to have a good time doing it. Make sure they realize that there is no totally right or totally wrong way to do the activity. Instead, they should listen closely to the scenarios that you lay out, think very quickly about how their assigned character would react to each, and then pretend to *be* that character to the best of their ability.

Choose the scenarios that you think your students will best understand. You may do one or two scenarios or all five. If you want, you can even make up new scenarios, with or without your students' help. Again, there is no right or wrong here. You are just moving the characters around a little bit in order to let students look at them a little differently and understand them a little bit better.

Read the scenario. Give students three to five minutes to prepare, and then give them five minutes to act out the scenario. The ONLY requirement is that students try as hard as possible to keep the character as he or she behaved in the book.

Scenario #1 Two students: Beatrice Hunsdorfer and a younger student
Beatrice has decided to go back to school and get her high school diploma. She has done her first writing assignment and has given it to another student to read over. The other student sees that Beatrice's writing has some flaws but is afraid of being rude to a person old enough to be her mother. Beatrice, for her part, wants desperately to learn and to improve but has no idea that she has trouble expressing herself in writing. After all, she thinks, she has no problem talking. ***Have the younger student critique Beatrice's paper honestly and have Beatrice respond accordingly.***

Character Exercise continued page 2

Scenario #2: Tillie and Ruth
Ruth has never been interested in science. Indeed, she has teased and ridiculed Tillie for her interest in atoms and other scientific issues. But suddenly Ruth's idol, Chris Burns, has decided to enter a project in the upcoming science fair. Now Ruth would also like to have a project to enter, but she has no idea where to begin. ***Have Ruth approach Tillie and ask her help in making an exhibit for the fair. Have Tillie respond.***

Scenario #3: Mr. Goodman and Beatrice
Beatrice has suddenly shown up in Mr. Goodman's office saying that she respects his opinion and wants to know what she should do to be a better parent to Ruth and Tillie. Her biggest concern is that she is not smart enough to be a good parent; his biggest concern is that he doesn't think she has the ability to be a good parent. But, of course, neither wants to be honest with the other. ***Have Beatrice and Mr. Goodman have a conversation about what makes a good parent and how Beatrice can become one.***

Scenario #4: Tillie and Ruth
After hearing about the famous Chris Burns from her sister for a long time, Tillie finally finds herself in the position of being paired with Chris in science class. They work on a project together and, amazingly enough, find that they have some things in common. After weeks of working on their project together, they begin to talk casually and to enjoy each other's company. Finally Chris asks Tillie to go to a school dance with him. Tillie knows how Ruth feels about Chris, but Chris has no idea that Ruth is especially attracted to him. Chris and Tillie both know that Chris has made fun of Tillie in the past. ***Have Chris ask Tillie to go to the dance with him and have Tillie respond.***

Lesson Thirteen

Objectives
1. To review Section 7
2. To do the pre-reading and reading for Section 8

Activity #1
Spend a short time reviewing the seventh section. See if students have any questions at this point.

Activity #2
Give students some time in class to do the pre-reading activities and the reading for Section 8.

Lesson Fourteen

Objectives
1. To review Section 8
2. To do the pre-reading and reading for Section 9

Activity #1
Spend a short time reviewing the eighth section.

Activity #2
Give students some time in class to do the pre-reading activities and the reading for Section 9.

Lesson Fifteen

Objectives
1. To review the main ideas and events in the entire play and to answer any remaining questions that students may have.
2. To have students exercise their critical thinking skills
3. To try to relate some of the ideas in **Marigolds** to the students' lives

Activity #1
Spend a short time making sure that students have understood the play. Try to get all remaining student questions out of the way before more formal discussion questions are introduced.

Activity #2
Choose the questions from the Extra Discussion Questions/Writing Assignments that seem most appropriate for your students. A class discussion of these questions is most effective if students have been given the opportunity to formulate answers to the questions prior to the discussion. To this end, you may either have all the students formulate answers to all of the questions, divide your class into groups and assign one or more questions to each group, or assign one question to each student in your class. The option you choose will obviously make a difference in the amount of class time needed for this activity.

Lesson Fifteen continued page 2

Activity #3
After students have had ample time to formulate answers to the questions, begin your class discussion of the questions and the ideas presented by the questions. Be sure students take notes during the discussion so they have information to study for the unit test.

Activity #4
Try to spend some time on the critical/personal response and personal response questions in order to give the students ways to think personally about the play's events, main ideas, and characters.

EXTRA DISCUSSION QUESTIONS/WRITING ASSIGNMENTS
The Effects of Gamma Rays on Man-in-the-Moon Marigolds

Interpretive
1. Where is the climax of the play? Explain your choice.

2. What is another possible title for the play? Explain your choice.

3. What are the main conflicts in the play, and how are they resolved?

4. What do you think are the three most important points that Paul Zindel tried to make in the play? Explain your choices.

5. How much time passes during the course of the play? Do you think that the amount of time covered has any significance?

6. Do you think that Paul Zindel likes any one character more than the others? Explain your answer based on the text.

Critical
7. Are the actions of the characters consistent? Explain why or why not?

8. Describe Tillie's relationship with her mother.

9. Describe Ruth's relationship with her mother.

10. Describe Ruth and Tillie's relationship with each other.

11. Does Beatrice have reason to be upset with her life? Explain.

12. In what way does the role of Nanny support the major themes of the play?

13. What is the effect of using characters like Mr. Goodman and Miss Hanley in the play but only showing them from the point of view of other characters?

14. Compare and contrast Tillie and Ruth.

15. Is the dialogue in the play believable? That is, do you think that the characters would actually talk as they do in the play?

16. Why did Ruth call her mother by the old nickname, Betty the Loon?

17. Who is the main character in the play? Defend your choice.

Extra Discussion Questions/Writing Assignments continued page 2

Critical/Personal Response

18. Are the characters in the play believable or not? Defend your position.

19. Is the plot of the play believable or not? Defend your position.

20. Explain what differences there might be in the way that audiences responded to the cigarette episodes in **Marigolds** in 1971 and how audiences might react today.

21. **Marigolds** is a very short play. Would it have been a better play if it had included perhaps another act or two or three?

22. If you were Ruth and Tillie, how would you have responded when you discovered the dead rabbit?

23. Who or what is responsible for Beatrice's situation in life?

Personal Response

24. Suppose you went to school with a person who was a little different and who was laughed at. How would you respond to that person?

25. How do you think a teacher and/or a principal should respond to a family that is having difficulties?

26. Is there any special value in being "different"?

27. Do schools today make students talented in certain areas feel left out of the mainstream of school life?

28. Did you enjoy reading **Marigolds**? Why or why not?

29. Have you read anything else by Paul Zindel? If so, were you surprised when you read **Marigolds** or did it seem like other Zindel works to you?

Quotations Name the speaker and the context and explain the significance of the quotation

1. "But most important, I suppose, my experiment has made me feel important- every atom in me, in everybody, has come from the sun-from places beyond our dreams."

2. "Tell them Mrs. Hunsdorfer called to thank them for making her wish she was dead...Would you give them that message, please?...Thank you very much."

Extra Discussion Questions/Writing Assignments continued page 3

3. "The only future plans I have for Tabby-my little brother asked the A.S.P.C.A. what its name was when he went to pick it up and they said it was called Tabby, but I think they were kidding him---

4. "And remember, I don't care even if you do win the whole damn thing, I'm not making any speech…."

5. "…The only time she ever made a fuss over me was when she drove me nuts."

6. "Mama, you look beautiful."

7. "That's what I call a half-life, Matilda! Me and cobalt-60! Two of the biggest half-lifes you ever saw!"

8. "No, I must admit that at this very moment I don't know what a mutation is…"

9. "Promise me you won't say anything."

10. "But…nobody laughed at me."

Lesson Sixteen

Objective
To complete the discussions begun in Lesson Fifteen

Activity
Since part of the previous lesson was taken up with giving students time to formulate answers to the discussion questions, you probably will need some additional time to complete your class discussions and to prepare students for the Unit Tests.

Note: Should your discussions be completed early, you could spend some time on project updates and/or just letting students ask any remaining questions they may have.

Lesson Seventeen

Objective
To review all of the vocabulary work done in this unit.

Activity
Choose one (or more) of the vocabulary review activities listed below and spend your class period as directed in the activity. Some of the materials for these review activities are located in the Vocabulary Resource section of this unit.

1. Divide your class into two teams and have an old-fashioned spelling or definition bee.

2. Give each of your students (or students in groups of two, three, or four) a Vocabulary Word Search Puzzle based on **Marigolds**. The person or group to find all of the vocabulary words in the puzzle first wins.

3. Give students a **Marigolds** Vocabulary Word Search Puzzle without the word list. The person or group to find the most vocabulary words in the puzzle wins.

4. Use a **Marigolds** Vocabulary Crossword Puzzle. Put a puzzle onto a transparency on the overhead projector so everyone can see it and do the puzzle together as a class.

5. Give students a **Marigolds** Vocabulary Matching Worksheet to do.

6. Divide your class into two teams. Use the **Marigolds** vocabulary words with their letters jumbled as a word list. Student 1 from Team A faces off against Student 1 from Team B. You write the first jumbled word on the board. The first student (1A or 1B) to unscramble the word wins the chance for his or her team to score points. If 1A wins the jumble, go to student 2A and give him or her a definition. He or she must give you the correct spelling of the vocabulary word which fits that definition. If he or she does, Team A scores a point, and you give student 3A a definition for which you expect a correctly spelled matching vocabulary word. Continu3 giving Team A definitions until some team member makes an incorrect response. An incorrect response sends the game back to the jumbled-word face off, this time with students 2A and 2B. Instead of repeating giving definitions to the first few students of each team, continue with the student after the one who gave the last incorrect response on the team. For example, if Team B wins the jumbled-word face-off and student 5B gave the last incorrect answer for Team B, you would start this round of definition questions with student 5B and so on. The team with the most points wins!

7. Have students write a story in which they correctly use as many vocabulary words as possible. Have students read their compositions orally! Post the most original compositions on your bulletin board.

Lesson Eighteen

Objective

To review the main ideas presented in **The Effects of Gamma Rays on Man-in-the-Moon Marigolds**

Activity #1

Choose one of the review games/activities included in the Extra Activities Packet and spend your class period as outlined there.

Activity #2

Remind students that the Unit Test will be given during the next class meeting. Stress the review of the Study Guides and their class notes as a last-minute, brush-up review for homework.

REVIEW GAMES/ACTIVITIES
The Effect of Gamma Rays on Man-in-the-Moon Marigolds

1. Ask the class to make up a unit test for **The Effect of Gamma Rays on Man-in- the-Moon Marigolds**. The test should have four sections: matching, short answer, multiple choice, and essay. Students may use half the period to make the test and then swap papers and use the other half of the class period to take a test a classmate has devised. The test should be taken open book. You may want to use the unit test included in this packet or take questions from the students' unit tests to formulate your own test.

2. Take half the period for students to make up short answer questions. Collect the questions. Divide the class into two teams. Alternate asking questions to individual members of teams A & B (like in a spelling bee). The question keeps going from A to B until it is correctly answered, then a new question is asked. A correct answer does not allow the team to get another question. Correct answers are +2 points; incorrect answers are -1 point.

3. Have students pair up and quiz each other from their study guides and class notes.

4. Give students a **Marigolds** crossword puzzle to complete.

5. Divide your class into two teams. Use the **Marigolds** crossword words with their letters jumbled as a word list. Student 1 from Team A faces off against Student 1 from Team B. You write the first jumbled word on the board. The first student (1A or 1B) to unscramble the word wins the chance for his or her team to score points. If 1A wins the jumble, go to student 2A and give him or her a clue. He or she must give you the correct word which matches that clue. If he or she does, Team A scores a point and you give student 3A a clue for which you expect another correct response. Continue giving Team A clues until some team member makes an incorrect response. An incorrect response sends the game back to the jumbled-word face-off, this time with students 2A and 2B. Instead of repeating giving clues to the first few students of each team, continue with the student after the one who gave the last incorrect response on the team. For example, if Team B wins the jumbled-word face-off and student 5B gave the last incorrect answer for Team B, you would start this round of clue questions with student 6B, and so on.

UNIT TESTS

SHORT ANSWER UNIT TEST #1
The Effect of Gamma Rays on Man-in-the-Moon Marigolds

I. Matching/Identify

1. ___ Tillie   A. the daughter who has convulsions

2. ___ Mr. Goodman   B. the school principal

3. ___ Beatrice   C. the school gym teacher

4. ___ Dr. Berg   D. the author of **Marigolds**

5. ___ Janice Vickery   E. the scientific daughter

6. ___ Paul Zindel   F. the science teacher

7. ___ Ruth   G. the girl who did the cat project

8. ___ Miss Hanley   H. the mother

II. Short Answer

1. On what does Tillie say that Mr. Goodman is going to do an experiment?

2. What is the history that Ruth refers to?

3. What have Tillie's marigold seeds been exposed to?

4. What new business does Beatrice say she is thinking of going into?

5. What one mistake does Beatrice say started her downfall?

6. What job is Ruth doing for Mr. Goodman?

7. What had Beatrice done with her father's wagon years ago?

Short Answer Unit Test #1 continued page 2

8. Who does Ruth say is Tillie's only competition at the science fair?

9. What does Tillie say about Beatrice's appearance when Beatrice appears at the top of the stairs all dressed up?

10. What does Tillie say is the most important thing her experiment has done?

III. Essay
What do you think are the three main points that Paul Zindel tries to make in the play? Explain your choices.

Short Answer Unit Test #1 continued page 3

IV. Vocabulary

Listen to the vocabulary word and spell it. After you have spelled all the words, go back and write down the definitions.

1.

2.

3.

4.

5.

6.

7.

8.

9.

10.

SHORT ANSWER UNIT TEST #2
The Effect of Gamma Rays on Man-in-the-Moon Marigolds

I. Matching/Identify

1. ___ Tillie   A. the girl who did the cat project

2. ___ Mr. Goodman   B. the science teacher

3. ___ Beatrice   C. the school gym teacher

4. ___ Dr. Berg   D. the author of **Marigolds**

5. ___ Janice Vickery   E. the mother

6. ___ Paul Zindel   F. the school principal

7. ___ Ruth   G. the daughter who has convulsions

8. ___ Miss Hanley   H. the scientific daughter

II. Short Answer

1. What was the small thing that Tillie says existed from the beginning of the world?

2. What are the two programs that Beatrice admits she never finished?

3. Why is Beatrice worried about Tillie's seeds?

4. What story does Ruth want Beatrice to tell her?

5. Whose face does Beatrice see in the window in her own nightmare?

6. What does Beatrice say she came up with when she took stock of her life?

7. What item of Tillie's clothing does Ruth say will make people laugh?

Short Answer Unit Test #2 continued page 2

8. What did Janice Vickery boil in a pot?

9. What does Ruth call Beatrice just as Beatrice starts to go out the door and get in the taxi?

10. What does Beatrice tell Tillie she hates?

III. Essay
Compare and contrast Tillie and Ruth.

Short Answer Unit Test #2 continued page 3

IV. Vocabulary

Listen to the vocabulary word and spell it. After you have spelled all the words, go back and write down the definitions.

1.

2.

3.

4.

5.

6.

7.

8.

9.

10.

KEY: SHORT ANSWER UNIT TESTS
The Effect of Gamma Rays on Man-in-the-Moon Marigolds

The short answer questions are taken directly from the study guides.
If you need to look up the answers, you will find them in the study guide section.

Answers to the composition questions will vary depending on your
class discussions and the level of your students.

For the vocabulary section of the test, choose ten of the
words from the vocabulary lists to read orally for your students.

The answers to the matching section of the test are below.

Answers to the matching section of the Advanced Short Answer Unit Test
are the same as for Short Answer Unit Test #2.

<u>Test #1</u>
1. E
2. F
3. H
4. B
5. G
6. D
7. A
8. C

<u>Test #2</u>
1. H
2. B
3. E
4. F
5. A
6. D
7. G
8. C

ADVANCED SHORT ANSWER UNIT TEST
The Effect of Gamma Rays on Man-in-the-Moon Marigolds

I   Matching/Identify

1. ___ Tillie   A. the girl who did the cat project

2. ___ Mr. Goodman   B. the science teacher

3. ___ Beatrice   C. the school gym teacher

4. ___ Dr. Berg   D. the author of **Marigolds**

5. ___ Janice Vickery   E. the mother

6. ___ Paul Zindel   F. the school principal

7. ___ Ruth   G. the daughter who has convulsions

8. ___ Miss Hanley   H. the scientific daughter

II.   Short Answer

1. Describe Tillie's relationship with her mother.

2. Describe Ruth's relationship with her mother.

3. Does Beatrice have reason to be upset with her life? Explain.

4. In what way does the role of Nanny support the major themes of the play?

Advanced Short Answer Unit Test continued page 2

5. What is the effect of using characters like Mr. Goodman and Miss Hanley in the play but only showing them from the point of view of other characters?

III. Quotations--Name the speaker and the context and explain the significance of the quotation:

1. "But most important, I suppose, my experiment has made me feel important-every atom in me, in everybody, has come from the sun-from places beyond our dreams."

2. "And remember, I don't care even if you do win the whole damn thing, I'm not making any speech…."

3. "…The only time she ever made a fuss over me was when she drove me nuts."

4. "That's what I call a half-life, Matilda! Me and cobalt-60! Two of the biggest half-lifes you ever saw!"

5. "Tell them Mrs. Hunsdorfer called to thank them for making her wish she was dead…Would you give them that message, please?…Thank you very much."

Advanced Short Answer Unit Test continued page 3

IV. Vocabulary

Define each of the vocabulary words below. After you have defined them all, write a paragraph in which you use all the words. The paragraph must in some way related to **Marigolds**.

1. inconspicuous
2. sinister
3. exasperate
4. smug
5. commences
6. primeval
7. ecstasy
8. pervades
9. saccharine
10. oblivious

Paragraph

MULTIPLE CHOICE-MATCHING UNIT TEST #1
The Effect of Gamma Rays on Man-in-the-Moon Marigolds

I. Matching/Identify

1. ___ Tillie   A. the daughter who has convulsions

2. ___ Mr. Goodman   B. the school principal

3. ___ Beatrice   C. the school gym teacher

4. ___ Dr. Berg   D. the author of **Marigolds**

5. ___ Janice Vickery   E. the scientific daughter

6. ___ Paul Zindel   F. the science teacher

7. ___ Ruth   G. the girl who did the cat project

8. ___ Miss Hanley   H. the mother

II. Multiple Choice
1. On what does Tillie say that Mr. Goodman is going to do an experiment?
    a. People's ability to withstand strain
    b. Stress in life
    c. Radioactivity
    d. Phases of the moon

2. What is the history that Ruth refers to?
    a. The story of her family's lives kept by the school
    b. The story of the family's happy past
    c. The stories told in her American history class
    d. the story Beatrice tells about her father's wagon

3. What have Tillie's marigold seeds been exposed to?
    a. Cat urine
    b. Cobalt-60
    c. Infrared lights
    d. Sunlight

Multiple Choice-Matching Unit Test #1 continued page 2

4. What new business does Beatrice say she is thinking of going into?
   a. A bed and breakfast
   b. A hotel
   c. A tea shop
   d. An old age home

5. What one mistake does Beatrice say started her downfall?
   a. She failed her beauty school course.
   b. She didn't finish high school.
   c. She married the wrong man and got tied down with children.
   d. She had a second child.

6. What job is Ruth doing for Mr. Goodman?
   a. She is babysitting his children.
   b. She is co-teaching a class with him.
   c. She is serving as a teacher's aide in his class.
   d. She is acting as Mr. Goodman's secretary.

7. What had Beatrice done with her father's wagon years ago?
   a. Burned it
   b. Ridden in it
   c. Gotten into it and driven it herself
   d. Steered it when her father got sick

8. Who does Ruth say is Tillie's only competition at the science fair?
   a. Chris Burns
   b. Miss Hanley
   c. Janice Vickery
   d. Herself

9. What does Tillie say about Beatrice's appearance when Beatrice appears at the top of the stairs all dressed up?
   a. "Gosh, Mama, are you really going to wear that!"
   b. "Come on, Mama, we're really late!"
   c. "Mama, you look beautiful."
   d. "Good heavens, Mama, not the feather boa, please!"

10. What does Tillie say is the most important thing her experiment has done?
    a. Tillie says her experiment has made her feel important.
    b. Tillie says her experiment has improved the whole world.
    c. Tillie says her experiment has made her mother happy.
    d. Tillie says her experiment has earned her an A+.

III. Essay

Which of the two daughters do you think Beatrice cares for the most and why?

Multiple Choice-Matching Unit Test #1 continued page 4

IV. Vocabulary

1.	misbegotten	A.	belonging to the first or earliest age
2.	ferment	B.	copied
3.	exasperate	C.	unaware of
4.	pathetic	D.	destructively violent; deranged; crazed
5.	triggers	E.	electromagnetic radiation
6.	vicious	F.	of dubious origin
7.	peculiar	G.	arousing sympathy and compassion
8.	berserk	H.	make angry or impatient
9.	smug	I.	structure of an organism or an organ
10.	gamma rays	J.	to seethe
11.	effeminate	K.	precipitates; causes to happen
12.	radioactivity	L.	savage; evil; dangerous
13.	atom	M.	odd
14.	sanatorium	N.	makes a disorderly search of
15.	bogey man	O.	self-satisfied; complacent
16.	rummages	P.	spontaneous emission of radiation
17.	primeval	Q.	smallest unit of an element
18.	mimeographed	R.	having qualities associated with women
19.	anatomy	S.	a place of convalescence from illness
20.	oblivious	T.	a terrifying presence; hobgoblin

MULTIPLE CHOICE-MATCHING UNIT TEST #2
The Effect of Gamma Rays on Man-in-the-Moon Marigolds

I. Matching/Identify

1. ___ Tillie   A. the girl who did the cat project

2. ___ Mr. Goodman   B. the science teacher

3. ___ Beatrice   C. the school gym teacher

4. ___ Dr. Berg   D. the author of **Marigolds**

5. ___ Janice Vickery   E. the mother

6. ___ Paul Zindel   F. the school principal

7. ___ Ruth   G. the daughter who has convulsions

8. ___ Miss Hanley   H. the scientific daughter

II. Multiple Choice

1. What was the small thing that Tillie says existed from the beginning of the world?
    a. Hope
    b. God
    c. Mankind
    d. An atom

2. What are the two programs that Beatrice admits she never finished?
    a. The real estate course and beauty school
    b. Study for her GED and the college prep course
    c. A business course and an accounting review for starting her own business
    d. A nursing course and a special session on aging

3. Why is Beatrice worried about Tillie's seeds?
    a. She thinks the rabbit will eat them.
    b. She thinks they will grow too big.
    c. She worries that they are stolen from the school
    d. She worries about their being radioactive.

Multiple Choice-Matching Unit Test #2 continued page 2

4. What story does Ruth want Beatrice to tell her?
   a. The story of the wagon
   b. Nice things about Ruth's father
   c. Old stories of how courageous Beatrice's father was during the war
   d. Stories about dead horses

5. Whose face does Beatrice see in the window in her own nightmare?
   a. Her dead father's
   b. A horse head
   c. Her mother smiling at her
   d. The man who sold her father fruit

6. What does Beatrice say she came up with when she took stock of her life?
   a. She came up with too much work to do by herself.
   b. She came up with a great plan to open a tea shop.
   c. She came up with "zero."
   d. She came up with a grand agenda.

7. What item of Tillie's clothing does Ruth say will make people laugh?
   a. Her jumper
   b. Her hair bow
   c. Her shoes
   d. Her raggy slip

8. What did Janice Vickery boil in a pot?
   a. A lobster
   b. Some kale
   c. A cat
   d. A rabbit

9. What does Ruth call Beatrice just as Beatrice starts to go out the door and get in the taxi?
   a. Mama, my beautiful Mama
   b. Pretty lady
   c. Betty the Loon
   d. You old biddy

10. What does Beatrice tell Tillie she hates?
    a. Both her and Ruth
    b. The world
    c. Mr. Goodman
    d. Chris Burns

III. Essay
Compare and contrast Tillie and Ruth.

Multiple Choice-Matching Unit Test #2 continued page 4

IV. Vocabulary

1.	misbegotten	A.	copied
2.	ferment	B.	of dubious origin
3.	exasperate	C.	unaware of
4.	pathetic	D.	destructively violent; deranged; crazed
5.	triggers	E.	electromagnetic radiation
6.	vicious	F.	belonging to the first or earliest age
7.	peculiar	G.	arousing sympathy and compassion
8.	berserk	H.	to seethe
9.	smug	I.	structure of an organism or an organ
10.	gamma rays	J.	make angry or impatient
11.	effeminate	K.	precipitates; causes to happen
12.	radioactivity	L.	a place of convalescence from illness
13.	atom	M.	self-satisfied; complacent
14.	sanatorium	N.	makes a disorderly search of
15.	bogey man	O.	odd
16.	rummages	P.	spontaneous emission of radiation
17.	primeval	Q.	smallest unit of an element
18.	mimeographed	R.	having qualities associated with women
19.	anatomy	S.	savage; evil; dangerous
20.	oblivious	T.	a terrifying presence; hobgoblin

ANSWER SHEET - *Marigolds*
Multiple Choice Unit Tests

I. Matching
1. ___
2. ___
3. ___
4. ___
5. ___
6. ___
7. ___
8. ___

II. Multiple Choice
1. ___
2. ___
3. ___
4. ___
5. ___
6. ___
7. ___
8. ___
9. ___
10. ___

IV. Vocabulary
1. ___
2. ___
3. ___
4. ___
5. ___
6. ___
7. ___
8. ___
9. ___
10. ___
11. ___
12. ___
13. ___
14. ___
15. ___
16. ___
17. ___
18. ___
19. ___
20. ___

ANSWER KEY MULTIPLE CHOICE UNIT TESTS
The Effect of Gamma Rays on Man-in-the-Moon Marigolds

Answers to Unit Test 1 are in the left column. Answers to Unit Test 2 are in the right column.

I. Matching	II. Multiple Choice	IV. Vocabulary
1. E H	1. C D	1. F B
2. F B	2. A A	2. J H
3. H E	3. B D	3. H J
4. B F	4. C A	4. G G
5. G A	5. C A	5. K K
6. D D	6. D C	6. L S
7. A G	7. C B	7. M O
8. C C	8. C C	8. D D
	9. C C	9. O M
	10. A A	10. E E
		11. R R
		12. P P
		13. Q Q
		14. S L
		15. T T
		16. N N
		17. A G
		18. B S
		19. I I
		20. C C

UNIT RESOURCES

BULLETIN BOARD IDEAS
The Effect of Gamma Rays on Man-in-the-Moon Marigolds

1. Have each student in the class choose a television or stage actor or actress to play each of the five characters (Beatrice, Tillie, Ruth, Janice Vickery, and Nanny) in the play. Then ask each student to write the name of each character on the card and next to it write his or her acting choice very clearly and carefully and explain briefly on the card why they think their actor or actress would be a good choice to play that character. Have each student tell the information on his or her card. Then post all of the index cards on the bulletin board. If your class is large and your bulletin board small, consider rotating the cards.

2. There is a lot of information available about Paul Zindel, the author of **Marigolds**. Have students research him and his work Then have each student choose one thing about Paul Zindel that he or she finds interesting. Put some brightly colored paper on the bulletin board and have students write in their most interesting piece of information about Paul Zindel. Be prepared yourself with some information and perhaps the names of his other works so that the information about him will be complete.

3. Make a kind of writing mural out of one bulletin board in your classroom. Invite students to use the board to express their personal feelings about the play. Ask students to take a minute at the beginning or end of each class period to write something that expresses their thoughts that day about the play, its ideas, its character, or its author. Set some guidelines about appropriateness of comments and then let students write whatever they want.

4. Save a portion of a black board to use as a bulletin board for rotating comments. Start each day with a comment that might be made by one of the three major characters in **Marigolds**. Sign your comment with the name of one of the characters. Invite students to make comments about the one you put up and sign their comment with the name of one of the other three characters. Try to build up some suspense every day about what comment will appear from which character. None of the comments need be from the book, only in character for the person making it.

5. Make a bulletin board listing the vocabulary words for this unit. As you complete sections of the play and discuss the vocabulary for each section, write the definitions on the bulletin board. Encourage students to look at the board often so that they learn the words easily.

6. With the permission of the student writers, post the best writing assignments done for this unit.

Bulletin Board Ideas continued page 2

7. If you have students who can draw, ask them to sketch a picture of one of the major characters or a scene from **Marigolds** and post it on the bulletin board.

8. Ask students to look through magazines and find pictures of people that look like their idea of each of the five characters in **Marigolds**. Get the students to post their pictures on the bulletin board labeled with the names of the characters the pictures make them think of. If you run short of material to cover one day, you could point to each picture on the bulletin board and see if there is consensus in the class about whether the pictures are like the characters or not. Even if the class disagrees with a particular association, that doesn't make the picture chosen wrong. It only means that a student has his or her own conception of what the character is like. Maybe that student will feel free to explain what he or she is thinking about the character. This might enlarge everyone's thoughts about the characters and the book.

EXTRA ACTIVITIES
The Effect of Gamma Rays on Man-in-the-Moon Marigolds

One of the difficulties in teaching a book is that not all students read at the same speed. One student who likes to read may take the book home and finish it in a day or two. Sometimes a few students finish the in-class assignments early. The problem, then, is finding suitable extra activities for students.

One useful thing to do is to keep a little library in the classroom. For this unit on **The Effect of Gamma Rays on Man-in-the-Moon Marigolds**, you might check out from the school or local library other related books and articles about child/parent relationships, radiation, starting a new business, caring for the elderly, rabbits, science fairs, etc. If possible, also have on hand some copies of Paul Zindel's other works so that students can read something else by the author if they choose to do so.

Other things you may keep on hand are puzzles. There are some in this unit directly relating to **Marigolds**. Feel free to duplicate them for your students' use.

Some students may like to draw or paint. You might devise a contest or allow some extra-credit grade for students who draw characters or scenes from **Marigolds.** Note, too, that if the students do not want to keep their drawings, you may pick up some extra bulletin board materials this way. If you have a contest and you supply the prize (a CD, a copy of another work by Zindel, a copy of a book on a subject similar to that in **Marigolds**, for example), you could possibly make the drawing itself a non-refundable entry fee. Make sure you assure students that you will continue to place their name on the board with the drawing. This can assure a student that years into the future his or her drawing will still be in his or her old classroom.

The pages which follow contain games, puzzles, and worksheets. The keys, when appropriate, immediately follow the puzzle or worksheet. There are two main groups of activities: one group for The unit; that is, generally relating to the text of **Marigolds**, and another group of activities related strictly to the vocabulary words in **Marigolds**.

Directions for these games, puzzles, and worksheets are self-explanatory. The object here is to provide you with extra materials you may use in any way you choose.

MORE ACTIVITIES
The Effect of Gamma Rays on Man-in-the-Moon Marigolds

1. Have students choose to "be" Beatrice, Tillie, or Ruth Hunsdorfer. Ask them to keep a journal daily in which they write about what happens to them-but in the voice and character of their chosen character. Everything they write in their journal should be done in character.

2. Encourage students to act out a few scenes of **Marigolds**. Although it is possible to teach a play mostly as a piece of literature, it is also useful to remind students that a play is written to be performed. Students could rehearse a few scenes and present them to the rest of the class. If they become practiced at it, they could even present the scenes to other classes in your school.

3. Encourage students to write one of the scenes in the book from the standpoint of Peter, the rabbit. This kind of exercise will make students look at the details of the book differently than they did on a first reading.

4. Have students pretend to be Beatrice, Tillie, or Ruth and ask them to write letters to Paul Zindel. In the letters they should try to get Zindel to rewrite all or parts of the play in order to significantly change their character.

5. Let interested students "teach" a class one day. If the number of interested students is sufficient, you could allow the students to work together, make a clear plan, and actually teach a whole class. Feel free to share your daily lesson plans with the students as they prepare to teach.

6. Have students design a CD cover for a piece of music that they think either Tillie or Ruth might like to make. They should name the piece of music and then design the cover in whatever way they think is appropriate.

7. Make a bulletin board with telephone numbers students can call for advice in case they want additional information about the subjects presented in **Marigolds**. For instance, if students wanted information about radioactivity, other scientific issues, raising regular marigolds, caring for a rabbit as a pet, starting a new business, licensure for real estate or other businesses, community standards regarding care of the elderly, etc., they would be able to gain easy access to it. Students might want this information for purposes of class or even for real life situations.

8. Ask students to pretend that someone from outer space has been deposited into the middle of the action presented in **Marigolds**. The students could pretend to be the alien and write a letter back to their planet describing the new world that they are observing.

More Activities continued page 2

9. Have students assume that they have become friends with any one of the major characters (Beatrice, Tillie, or Ruth) in the play. The students should write a paper or have a discussion regarding the type of gift they would like to give to their chosen character and why.

10. Have students discuss which television show they believe would be the favorite of each of the major characters in the play.

11. Students could consider whether they would like to be Beatrice's son or daughter. Have them explain why or why not they believe she would be a good parent.

12. Students could create original costumes for one or two of the characters in **Marigolds**. A costume could actually be made and modeled or a few costume designs could be drawn and posted around the classroom.

WORD SEARCH
The Effect of Gamma Rays on Man-in-the-Moon Marigolds

Words are placed backwards, forward, diagonally, up and down. Clues listed below can help you find the words.
Circle the hidden vocabulary words in the maze.

```
B E A T R I C E D I X O R D Y H D T E A
E E P K Z A C G Z Q D Y R W U N N I P J
A H R R O I D Y E G N A B N A E L C E V
U A P G N O F I G S P M S H R A I K T Y
T N S A C N L H O N T D L E B T P I E R
I L J E U A N S A A O A F O W O S N R M
F E M C C L T M D R C F P H O M T G M V
U Y A H L R D A F A I T Y O L N I W A B
L G R K C O E R D U T I K M S C H T H
Q G I K O S R T T A U G M V C K K G I R
L A G G C T Z V A D C L H T I Y C N L Q
S R O L F W V T J R H T V T W T N N D L
S D L O G I R A M G Y Y S K E N Y Z A Y
R B D C O N V U L S I O N S K R G G G V
E X P E R I M E N T S Z N Z T V C X H P
```

American plants with yellow or orange flowers
Beatrice says the world kills off people who are ___.
Beatrice's last name
Devil's Kiss is a type of ____.
German security police during Nazi regime
Going to the bathroom is Nanny's ____.
In high school Beatrice was called Betty the ___.
Janice boiled the cat in sodium ___ solution.
Kind of shop Beatrice wants to open
Mr. Goodman is doing an experiment on ___.
Nanny has what in her eyes?
Nanny was left with Beatrice by her ___.
Nanny's movements are like a ____ clock.
Part of Tillie's body that came from a star

Ruth has nightmares about Mr. ___.
Ruth is Mr. Goodman's ___.
Ruth's biggest problem is that she has ___.
Ruth's favorite cigarettes are ___.
Small thing that existed since the beginning of the world
The Principal's name is Dr. ___.
The author of MARIGOLDS is ___ Zindel.
The girl who did the cat project was ___ Vickery.
The gym teacher's name is Miss ___.
The mother in the book
The rabbit's name
The science teacher was Mr. ____.
Tillie is raising ____ seeds.
Tillie likes to do ____.
Tillie tells her mother, 'Mama, you look ___.'
Tillie's real name
What Tillie's slip was

ANSWER KEY
The Effect of Gamma Rays on Man-in-the-Moon Marigolds

```
B E A T R I C E D I X O R D Y H D T E A
E E   K   A C G       Y     U N N I P
A H R   O I D   E     A   N A E L C E
U A P G N O   I   S   M S H R A I K T
T N S A C   L   O N T D L E   T P I E
I L J E U A   S A A O A F O   O S N R
F E M   C L T M D R C F P   O M T G M
U Y A     R D A F A I T Y O   N I   A
L G R     O E E R D U T I     C   T
  G I   O   R T   A U G V   K   I
  A G G         A D C   H   I       L
  R O             R   T   T     D
S D L O G I R A M   Y   S   E   Y A
    D C O N V U L S I O N S   R
E X P E R I M E N T S
```

Effect of Gamma Rays on Man in the Moon Marigolds Crossword

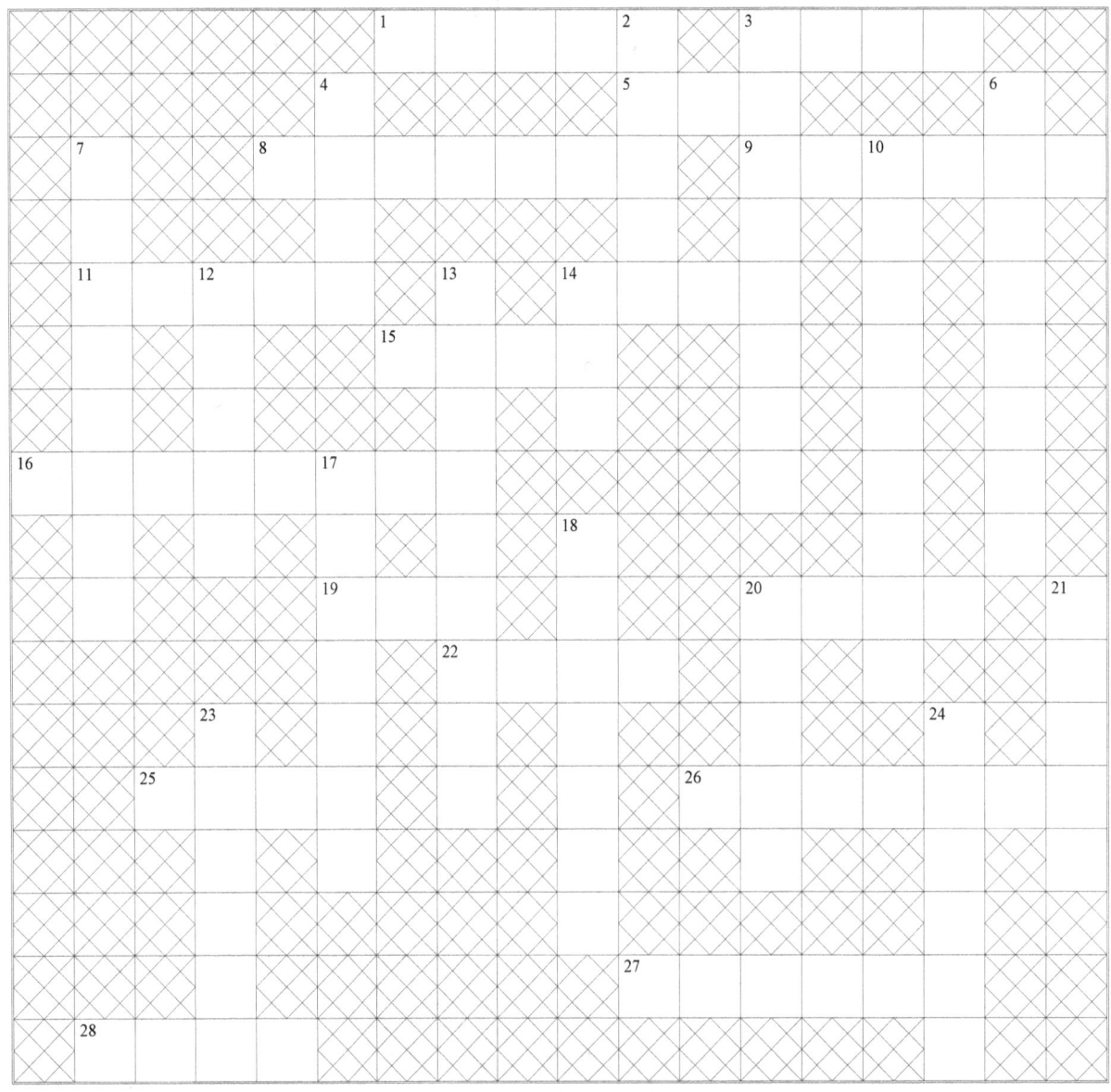

Across
1. Ruth's favorite cigarettes are ____.
3. Ruth has nightmares about Mr. ____.
5. Kind of shop Beatrice wants to open
8. Tillie's real name
9. Beatrice killed it
11. Beatrice told Tillie she hates the ___
14. Principal's name: Dr. ____.
15. When Beatrice took stock of her life, she came up with ___
16. Nanny was left with Beatrice by her ____.
19. Janice Vickery boiled one in a pot
20. Author: ____ Zindel
22. Small thing that existed since the beginning of the world
25. In high school Beatrice was called Betty the ____.
26. German security police during Nazi regime
27. Girl who did the cat project: ____ Vickery
28. Going to the bathroom is Nanny's ____.

Down
2. Beatrice is invited to sit there with mothers of the other finalists
3. Tillie is raising ____ seeds.
4. Part of Tillie's body that came from a star
6. Ruth and Beatrice share ___ and cigarettes.
7. Beatrice says her ___ started when she married the wrong man
10. Tillie tells her mother,
12. What Tillie's slip was
13. Ruth is Mr. Goodman's ____.
14. Ruth says Tillie's hair ___ will make people laugh
17. Nanny's movements are like a ____ clock.
18. Science teacher
20. Rabbit's name
21. Beatrice tells Ruth the story of the ___
23. Marigold seeds were exposed to ___-60
24. Gym tea

Effect of Gamma Rays on Man in the Moon Marigolds Crossword Answer Key

					¹K	O	O	L	²S		³M	A	Y	O	
				⁴H					⁵T	E	A			⁶L	
	⁷D		⁸M	A	T	I	L	D	A		⁹R	A	¹⁰B	I	T
	O			N					G		I		E		P
¹¹W	O	¹²R	L	D		¹³S		¹⁴B	E	R	G		A		S
	N		A		¹⁵Z	E	R	O			O		U		T
	F		G			C		W			L		T		I
¹⁶D	A	U	G	¹⁷T	E	R					D		I		C
	L		Y		I			¹⁸G			F		K	
	L			¹⁹C	A	T		O		²⁰P	A	U	L		²¹W
				K			²²A	T	O	M	E		L		A
		²³C		I			R		D		T		²⁴H		G
		²⁵L	O	O	N		Y		M		²⁶G	E	S	T	A	P	O
				B		G		A			R			N		N
				A				N						L	
				L				²⁷J	A	N	I	C	E	
		²⁸D	U	T	Y									Y	

Across
1. Ruth's favorite cigarettes are ____.
3. Ruth has nightmares about Mr. ____.
5. Kind of shop Beatrice wants to open
8. Tillie's real name
9. Beatrice killed it
11. Beatrice told Tillie she hates the ___
14. Principal's name: Dr. ____.
15. When Beatrice took stock of her life, she came up with ___
16. Nanny was left with Beatrice by her ____.
19. Janice Vickery boiled one in a pot
20. Author: ____ Zindel
22. Small thing that existed since the beginning of the world
25. In high school Beatrice was called Betty the ____.
26. German security police during Nazi regime
27. Girl who did the cat project: ____ Vickery
28. Going to the bathroom is Nanny's ____.

Down
2. Beatrice is invited to sit there with mothers of the other finalists
3. Tillie is raising ____ seeds.
4. Part of Tillie's body that came from a star
6. Ruth and Beatrice share ___ and cigarettes.
7. Beatrice says her ___ started when she married the wrong man
10. Tillie tells her mother,
12. What Tillie's slip was
13. Ruth is Mr. Goodman's ____.
14. Ruth says Tillie's hair ___ will make people laugh
17. Nanny's movements are like a ____ clock.
18. Science teacher
20. Rabbit's name
21. Beatrice tells Ruth the story of the ___
23. Marigold seeds were exposed to ___-60
24. Gym teacher

MATCHING QUIZ/WORKSHEET 1 - The Effect of Gamma Rays on Man-in-the-Moon Marigolds

___ 1. PETER   A. Ruth says Tillie's hair ___ will make people laugh
___ 2. EXPERIMENTS   B. Ruth and Beatrice share ___ and cigarettes.
___ 3. GESTAPO   C. The mother in the book
___ 4. FAIR   D. Nanny was left with Beatrice by her ____.
___ 5. CHRIS   E. Ruth's favorite cigarettes are ____.
___ 6. WORLD   F. Gym teacher
___ 7. BEATRICE   G. Beatrice told Tillie she hates the ___
___ 8. MARIGOLD   H. Tillie is raising ____ seeds.
___ 9. BOW   I. Nanny's movements are like a ____ clock.
___ 10. DAUGHTER   J. Going to the bathroom is Nanny's ____.
___ 11. HUNSDORFER   K. German security police during Nazi regime
___ 12. RABBIT   L. Ruth has nightmares about Mr. ____.
___ 13. LIPSTICK   M. Tillie likes to them
___ 14. TICKING   N. Girl who did the cat project: ____ Vickery
___ 15. SECRETARY   O. Beatrice killed it
___ 16. DUTY   P. Ruth tells Beatrice that Tillie is one of the finalists in the science ___
___ 17. COBALT   Q. Rabbit's name
___ 18. BEAUTIFUL   R. Mr. Goodman is doing an experiment on ____
___ 19. BERG   S. Marigold seeds were exposed to ___-60
___ 20. MAYO   T. Janice boiled the cat in sodium ____ solution.
___ 21. KOOLS   U. Tillie tells her mother,
___ 22. HANLEY   V. Beatrice's last name
___ 23. RADIOACTIVITY W. Ruth is worried about being embarrassed in front of ___ Burns.
___ 24. HYDROXIDE   X. Principal's name: Dr. ____.
___ 25. JANICE   Y. Ruth is Mr. Goodman's ____.

KEY : MATCHING QUIZ/WORKSHEET 1 - The Effect of Gamma Rays on Man-in-the-Moon Marigolds

Q - 1.	PETER	A.	Ruth says Tillie's hair ___ will make people laugh
M - 2.	EXPERIMENTS	B.	Ruth and Beatrice share ___ and cigarettes.
K - 3.	GESTAPO	C.	The mother in the book
P - 4.	FAIR	D.	Nanny was left with Beatrice by her ____.
W - 5.	CHRIS	E.	Ruth's favorite cigarettes are ____.
G - 6.	WORLD	F.	Gym teacher
C - 7.	BEATRICE	G.	Beatrice told Tillie she hates the ___
H - 8.	MARIGOLD	H.	Tillie is raising ____ seeds.
A - 9.	BOW	I.	Nanny's movements are like a ____ clock.
D - 10.	DAUGHTER	J.	Going to the bathroom is Nanny's ____.
V - 11.	HUNSDORFER	K.	German security police during Nazi regime
O - 12.	RABBIT	L.	Ruth has nightmares about Mr. ____.
B - 13.	LIPSTICK	M.	Tillie likes to them
I - 14.	TICKING	N.	Girl who did the cat project: ____ Vickery
Y - 15.	SECRETARY	O.	Beatrice killed it
J - 16.	DUTY	P.	Ruth tells Beatrice that Tillie is one of the finalists in the science ___
S - 17.	COBALT	Q.	Rabbit's name
U - 18.	BEAUTIFUL	R.	Mr. Goodman is doing an experiment on ____
X - 19.	BERG	S.	Marigold seeds were exposed to ___-60
L - 20.	MAYO	T.	Janice boiled the cat in sodium ____ solution.
E - 21.	KOOLS	U.	Tillie tells her mother,
F - 22.	HANLEY	V.	Beatrice's last name
R - 23.	RADIOACTIVITY	W.	Ruth is worried about being embarrassed in front of ___ Burns.
T - 24.	HYDROXIDE	X.	Principal's name: Dr. ____.
N - 25.	JANICE	Y.	Ruth is Mr. Goodman's ____.

MATCHING QUIZ/WORKSHEET 2 - The Effect of Gamma Rays on Man-in-the-Moon Marigolds

___ 1. LIPSTICK   A. Janice Vickery boiled one in a pot
___ 2. STAGE   B. Beatrice says her ___ started when she married the wrong man
___ 3. RABBIT   C. German security police during Nazi regime
___ 4. ATOM   D. Author: ___ Zindel
___ 5. LOON   E. The mother in the book
___ 6. TEA   F. Tillie likes to them
___ 7. EXPERIMENTS   G. Girl who did the cat project: ___ Vickery
___ 8. BEATRICE   H. Going to the bathroom is Nanny's ___.
___ 9. DOWNFALL   I. When Beatrice took stock of her life, she came up with ___
___10. COBALT   J. What Tillie's slip was
___11. TICKING   K. Marigold seeds were exposed to ___-60
___12. HAND   L. Ruth is Mr. Goodman's ___.
___13. ZERO   M. Principal's name: Dr. ___.
___14. DUTY   N. Small thing that existed since the beginning of the world
___15. GESTAPO   O. Beatrice is invited to sit there with mothers of the other finalists
___16. PAUL   P. Ruth and Beatrice share ___ and cigarettes.
___17. RAGGY   Q. Beatrice told Tillie she hates the ___
___18. JANICE   R. In high school Beatrice was called Betty the ___.
___19. WORLD   S. Ruth is worried about being embarrassed in front of ___ Burns.
___20. CAT   T. Beatrice says the world kills off people who are ___.
___21. HUNSDORFER   U. Beatrice's last name
___22. CHRIS   V. Part of Tillie's body that came from a star
___23. BERG   W. Kind of shop Beatrice wants to open
___24. DIFFERENT   X. Beatrice killed it
___25. SECRETARY   Y. Nanny's movements are like a ___ clock.

KEY : MATCHING QUIZ/WORKSHEET 2 - The Effect of Gamma Rays on Man-in-the-Moon Marigolds

P - 1. LIPSTICK	A.	Janice Vickery boiled one in a pot
O - 2. STAGE	B.	Beatrice says her ___ started when she married the wrong man
X - 3. RABBIT	C.	German security police during Nazi regime
N - 4. ATOM	D.	Author: ____ Zindel
R - 5. LOON	E.	The mother in the book
W - 6. TEA	F.	Tillie likes to them
F - 7. EXPERIMENTS	G.	Girl who did the cat project: ____ Vickery
E - 8. BEATRICE	H.	Going to the bathroom is Nanny's ____.
B - 9. DOWNFALL	I.	When Beatrice took stock of her life, she came up with ___
K -10. COBALT	J.	What Tillie's slip was
Y -11. TICKING	K.	Marigold seeds were exposed to ___-60
V -12. HAND	L.	Ruth is Mr. Goodman's ____.
I -13. ZERO	M.	Principal's name: Dr. ____.
H -14. DUTY	N.	Small thing that existed since the beginning of the world
C -15. GESTAPO	O.	Beatrice is invited to sit there with mothers of the other finalists
D -16. PAUL	P.	Ruth and Beatrice share ___ and cigarettes.
J -17. RAGGY	Q.	Beatrice told Tillie she hates the ___
G -18. JANICE	R.	In high school Beatrice was called Betty the ____.
Q -19. WORLD	S.	Ruth is worried about being embarrassed in front of ___ Burns.
A -20. CAT	T.	Beatrice says the world kills off people who are ____.
U -21. HUNSDORFER	U.	Beatrice's last name
S -22. CHRIS	V.	Part of Tillie's body that came from a star
M -23. BERG	W.	Kind of shop Beatrice wants to open
T -24. DIFFERENT	X.	Beatrice killed it
L -25. SECRETARY	Y.	Nanny's movements are like a ____ clock.

JUGGLE LETTER REVIEW GAME
The Effect of Gamma Rays on Man-in-the-Moon Marigolds

DNHA	HAND	Part of Tillie's body that came from a star
MTOA	ATOM	Small thing that existed since the beginning of the world
ATLAMDI	MATILDA	Tillie's real name
ITAYVROADICIT	RADIOACTIVITY	Mr. Goodman is doing an experiment on ____
GAYGR	RAGGY	What Tillie's slip was
KLISITCP	LIPSTICK	Devil's Kiss is a type of ____.
EAT	TEA	Kind of shop Beatrice wants to open
RAMODGLI	MARIGOLD	Tillie is raising ____ seeds.
SOLOK	KOOLS	Ruth's favorite cigarettes are ___.
RACASTTCA	CATARACTS	Nanny has what in her eyes?
CAEJIN	JANICE	The girl who did the cat project was ___ Vickery.
OMODANG	GOODMAN	The science teacher was Mr. ____.
KINGCIT	TICKING	Nanny's movements are like a ____ clock.
TUYD	DUTY	Going to the bathroom is Nanny's ____.
CERRASYTE	SECRETARY	Ruth is Mr. Goodman's ___.
RERONDHUFS	HUNSDORFER	Beatrice's last name
YELANH	HANLEY	The gym teacher's name is Miss ___.
GREB	BERG	The Principal's name is Dr. ___.
LUPA	PAUL	The author of *Marigolds* is ___ Zindel.
YMOA	MAYO	Ruth has nightmares about Mr. ___.
ONLO	LOON	In high school Beatrice was called Betty the ___.
ILFUEABUT	BEAUTIFUL	Tillie tells her mother, "Mama, you look ____."
FEEDNTRIF	DIFFERENT	Beatrice says the world kills off people who are ___.
DXODYHIER	HYDROXIDE	Janice boiled the cat in sodium ___ solution.
THADREUG	DAUGHTER	Nanny was left with Beatrice by her ____.
TEGOPAS	GESTAPO	German security police during Nazi regime
SNCVUOSINOL	CONVULSIONS	Ruth's biggest problem is that she has ___.
SLAMIRDOG	MARIGOLDS	American plants with yellow or orange flowers
BICEERAT	BEATRICE	The mother in the book
EIPSRTENEMX	EXPERIMENTS	Tillie likes to do ____.
TREEP	PETER	The rabbit's name

VOCABULARY RESOURCES

VOCABULARY WORD SEARCH
The Effect of Gamma Rays on Man-in-the-Moon Marigolds

Words are placed backwards, forward, diagonally, up and down. Clues listed below can help you find the words. Circle the hidden vocabulary words in the maze.

```
C I T E H T A P C H L O R O F O R M S M
A O G C X S U R V E Y S B E C E C E N U
L E M S V A V B T N B S R L T C G O O T
C A I P J B S M U G K M T S I A J Y O A
U V M S E R O P V R E H I E M V S K P T
L E E A M T U K E N S N O M R A I Z S I
A S O G A T I S T R I T U R T I S O S O
T D G Y X H R T T S A R A S R U C I U N
E R R T D E A E I L N T C G O I S A Y S
S O A I B E I R M O I E E L G A F M L K
B P P N V N L I O B N N A V I E O I G D
X P H R L N U L Y V L E G R Y T R L E Y
L I E E P J C I L H J E O Q A F M I V S
N N D T H D E T R G W S H N S T P Y N B
J G P E F S P Y V F P L A V E M I R P G
```

A change, as in nature, form, or quality
A skin disease
An eccentric person
Arousing sympathy and compassion
Belonging to the first or earliest age or ages
Brazen boldness
Computes mathematically
Continuance without beginning or end
Copied
Deranged; crazed
Envious
Examines; looks at comprehensively
Having excessive or uncontrollable emotion
Incapability of producing offspring
Intense joy or delight
Listening secretly

Make angry or impatient
Makes a disorderly search of
Odd
One who is crazy or simple-minded
One who pries secretly
Others capable of winning
Overwhelming
Scares; shocks; causes horror
Self-satisfied; complacent
Shake violently
Sharp breaths
Smallest unit of an element
Soft fluttering or crackling sounds
Structure of an organism or organ
Threatening evil
To anesthetize or kill with chloroform
To seethe; to be agitated
Unaware of

VOCABULARY ANSWER KEYS
The Effect of Gamma Rays on Man-in-the-Moon Marigolds

```
C I T E H T A P C H L O R O F O R M S M
A O     X S U R V E Y S B E   E C E N U
L E M S   A         S R L T   G O O T
C A I P     S M U G K M T S I A   Y O A
U V M S E R O P   R E H I E M V S   P T
L E E A   T U   E N S N O M R A I     I
A S O G A T I S T R I T U R T I S O S O
T D G Y     R T T S A R A S R U C I U N
E R R T   E A E I L N T C G O I S A Y S
S O A I B E I R M O I E E L G A F M L
  P P N V   L I O B N N A   I E O I
    P H R     U L     L E G R   T R   E
    I E E     C I     J E O   A   I     S
    N D T     E T       S   N         N
    G   E     P Y     P L A V E M I R P G
```

Effect of Gamm Rays on Man in the Moon Marigolds Vocabulary Crosswerd

Across
1. Make angry or impatient
9. To seethe; to be agitated
10. Time for half of nuclei to radioactively decay
12. Chemical to anesthetize or kill
14. Self-satisfied; complacent
17. Continuance without beginning or end
18. One who is crazy or simple-minded
24. Intense involuntary muscular contractions
26. Smallest unit of an element
27. A terrifying presence; hobgoblin
28. Savage; evil; dangerous

Down
2. Kill by preventing access to oxygen
3. Structure of an organism or organ
4. Having qualities usually associated with females
5. Precipitates; causes to happen
6. Brazen boldness
7. Overwhelming
8. Blood clot in blood vessel or heart
11. An eccentric person
13. Having excessive or uncontrollable emotion
15. Sharp breaths
16. Others capable of winning
19. Very old
20. A change, as in nature, form, or quality
21. One who pries secretly
22. Shake violently
23. Deranged; crazed
25. Examines; looks at comprehensively

Effect of Gamma Rays on Man in the Moon Marigolds Vocabulary Crossword Answer Key

		1 E	X	2 A	S	P	E	3 R	A	4 T	E		5 T		6 N		7 S
	8 T			U				A				9 F	E	R	M	E	N	T
	10 H	A	L	F	L	I	F	E		A		F		I		R		A
	R			F		11 C		T		E		I		G		V		G
	O	12 C	13 H	L	O	R	O	F	O	R	M		G		E		G
14 S	M	U	15 G		Y		C		O		M		I		E			E
	B		A		S		A		T		Y		N		R		16 C	
	O		S		T		17 E	T	E	R	N	I	T	Y		18 L	O	O	N
	S		P		E		R						Y				E		M	G
	I		S		R		19 A		20 M				21 S			P	
22 T		23 B		24 C	O	N	V	U	L	S	I	O	N	S		E	
R		E		A		C		T		U			O		26 A	T	O	M
E		R		L		I		A		R			O		I		
M		S		E		T		V			O		P		T	
27 B	O	G	E	Y	M	A	N		I		E				I	
L		R				T		O		28 V	I	C	I	O	U	S
E		K				N		S							N	

Across
1. Make angry or impatient
9. To seethe; to be agitated
10. Time for half of nuclei to radioactively decay
12. Chemical to anesthetize or kill
14. Self-satisfied; complacent
17. Continuance without beginning or end
18. One who is crazy or simple-minded
24. Intense involuntary muscular contractions
26. Smallest unit of an element
27. A terrifying presence; hobgoblin
28. Savage; evil; dangerous

Down
2. Kill by preventing access to oxygen
3. Structure of an organism or organ
4. Having qualities usually associated with females
5. Precipitates; causes to happen
6. Brazen boldness
7. Overwhelming
8. Blood clot in blood vessel or heart
11. An eccentric person
13. Having excessive or uncontrollable emotion
15. Sharp breaths
16. Others capable of winning
19. Very old
20. A change, as in nature, form, or quality
21. One who pries secretly
22. Shake violently
23. Deranged; crazed
25. Examines; looks at comprehensively

VOCABULARY WORKSHEET 1 - The Effect of Gamma Rays on Man-in-the-Moon Marigolds

___ 1. HYSTERICAL   A. Very old
___ 2. EXAGGERATING   B. Time for half of nuclei to radioactively decay
___ 3. RUSTLING   C. Threatening evil
___ 4. HALFLIFE   D. Enlarging, increasing beyond normal bounds
___ 5. TREMBLE   E. Blood clot in blood vessel or heart
___ 6. RADIOACTIVITY   F. One who pries secretly
___ 7. SILHOUETTE   G. Emphasizes
___ 8. SANATORIUM   H. Structure of an organism or organ
___ 9. NERVE   I. Like a machine
___10. ANATOMY   J. Outline or profile
___11. MUTATION   K. Brazen boldness
___12. OBLIVIOUS   L. Stressed; accented
___13. SNOOP   M. Sliding feet along the floor
___14. VIBRATES   N. A change, as in nature, form, or quality
___15. ACCENTUATED   O. Shakes or trembles
___16. SHUFFLING   P. Having excessive or uncontrollable emotion
___17. BOGEYMAN   Q. Spontaneous emission of radiation
___18. THROMBOSIS   R. Listening secretly
___19. EAVESDROPPING   S. A terrifying presence; hobgoblin
___20. ANCIENT   T. Continuance without beginning or end
___21. ETERNITY   U. A place of convalescence from illness
___22. SINISTER   V. Soft fluttering or crackling sounds
___23. MECHANICALLY   W. Having qualities usually associated with females
___24. EFFEMINATE   X. Shake violently
___25. PUNCTUATES   Y. Unaware of

KEY: VOCABULARY WORKSHEET 1 - The Effect of Gamma Rays on Man-in-the-Moon Marigolds

P - 1.	HYSTERICAL	A. Very old
D - 2.	EXAGGERATING	B. Time for half of nuclei to radioactively decay
V - 3.	RUSTLING	C. Threatening evil
B - 4.	HALFLIFE	D. Enlarging, increasing beyond normal bounds
X - 5.	TREMBLE	E. Blood clot in blood vessel or heart
Q - 6.	RADIOACTIVITY	F. One who pries secretly
J - 7.	SILHOUETTE	G. Emphasizes
U - 8.	SANATORIUM	H. Structure of an organism or organ
K - 9.	NERVE	I. Like a machine
H - 10.	ANATOMY	J. Outline or profile
N - 11.	MUTATION	K. Brazen boldness
Y - 12.	OBLIVIOUS	L. Stressed; accented
F - 13.	SNOOP	M. Sliding feet along the floor
O - 14.	VIBRATES	N. A change, as in nature, form, or quality
L - 15.	ACCENTUATED	O. Shakes or trembles
M - 16.	SHUFFLING	P. Having excessive or uncontrollable emotion
S - 17.	BOGEYMAN	Q. Spontaneous emission of radiation
E - 18.	THROMBOSIS	R. Listening secretly
R - 19.	EAVESDROPPING	S. A terrifying presence; hobgoblin
A - 20.	ANCIENT	T. Continuance without beginning or end
T - 21.	ETERNITY	U. A place of convalescence from illness
C - 22.	SINISTER	V. Soft fluttering or crackling sounds
I - 23.	MECHANICALLY	W. Having qualities usually associated with females
W - 24.	EFFEMINATE	X. Shake violently
G - 25.	PUNCTUATES	Y. Unaware of

VOCABULARY WORKSHEET 2 - The Effect of Gamma Rays on Man-in-the-Moon Marigolds

___ 1. RADIOACTIVITY   A. Sliding feet along the floor
___ 2. BERSERK   B. An eccentric person
___ 3. PECULIAR   C. Spreads throughout
___ 4. SILHOUETTE   D. Spontaneous emission of radiation
___ 5. INCONSPICUOUS   E. Envious
___ 6. PATHETIC   F. Having excessive or uncontrollable emotion
___ 7. PSORIASIS   G. Structure of an organism or organ
___ 8. RUSTLING   H. Odd
___ 9. BOGEYMAN   I. Uproot and replant
___10. TRANSPLANT   J. Makes a disorderly search of
___11. JEALOUS   K. Outline or profile
___12. MISBEGOTTEN   L. Arousing sympathy and compassion
___13. MECHANICALLY   M. Not readily noticeable
___14. SHUFFLING   N. Deranged; crazed
___15. CHLOROFORM   O. A skin disease
___16. COMMENCES   P. Chemical to anesthetize or kill
___17. CATARACTS   Q. A terrifying presence; hobgoblin
___18. COOT   R. Soft fluttering or crackling sounds
___19. PERVADES   S. Of dubious origins
___20. HYSTERICAL   T. Opacities of the eye lens or capsule
___21. THROMBOSIS   U. Blood clot in blood vessel or heart
___22. RUMMAGES   V. Starts
___23. ANATOMY   W. Sharp breaths
___24. GASPS   X. Emphasizes
___25. PUNCTUATES   Y. Like a machine

KEY: VOCABULARY WORKSHEET 2 - The Effect of Gamma Rays on Man-in-the-Moon Marigolds

D - 1.	RADIOACTIVITY	A. Sliding feet along the floor
N - 2.	BERSERK	B. An eccentric person
H - 3.	PECULIAR	C. Spreads throughout
K - 4.	SILHOUETTE	D. Spontaneous emission of radiation
M - 5.	INCONSPICUOUS	E. Envious
L - 6.	PATHETIC	F. Having excessive or uncontrollable emotion
O - 7.	PSORIASIS	G. Structure of an organism or organ
R - 8.	RUSTLING	H. Odd
Q - 9.	BOGEYMAN	I. Uproot and replant
I - 10.	TRANSPLANT	J. Makes a disorderly search of
E - 11.	JEALOUS	K. Outline or profile
S - 12.	MISBEGOTTEN	L. Arousing sympathy and compassion
Y - 13.	MECHANICALLY	M. Not readily noticeable
A - 14.	SHUFFLING	N. Deranged; crazed
P - 15.	CHLOROFORM	O. A skin disease
V - 16.	COMMENCES	P. Chemical to anesthetize or kill
T - 17.	CATARACTS	Q. A terrifying presence; hobgoblin
B - 18.	COOT	R. Soft fluttering or crackling sounds
C - 19.	PERVADES	S. Of dubious origins
F - 20.	HYSTERICAL	T. Opacities of the eye lens or capsule
U - 21.	THROMBOSIS	U. Blood clot in blood vessel or heart
J - 22.	RUMMAGES	V. Starts
G - 23.	ANATOMY	W. Sharp breaths
W 24.	GASPS	X. Emphasizes
X - 25.	PUNCTUATES	Y. Like a machine

VOCABULARY JUGGLE LETTER REVIEW GAME - MARIGOLDS

GOMBTSEINET	MISBEGOTTEN	Of dubious origins
NEETRFM	FERMENT	To seethe; to be agitated
TEFFNIEEAM	EFFEMINATE	Having qualities usually associated with females
MALVRIPE	PRIMEVAL	Belonging to the first or earliest age or ages
GASTIGENRG	STAGGERING	Overwhelming
MOTA	ATOM	Smallest unit of an element
CIRPELUA	PECULIAR	Odd
IDTVYIARITOAC	RADIOACTIVITY	Spontaneous emission of radiation
MOOHLFCORR	CHLOROFORM	To anesthetize or kill with chloroform
GXIGARGENATE	EXAGGERATING	Enlarging, increasing beyond normal bounds
TOCO	COOT	An eccentric person
STEYSAC	ECSTASY	Intense joy or delight
POASSIRIS	PSORIASIS	A skin disease
LIGNFIGN	FLINGING	Casting aside; discarding
TEYRINET	ETERNITY	Continuance without beginning or end
TSANNALPTR	TRANSPLANT	Uproot and replant
LAESUCCALT	CALCULATES	Computes mathematically
SRUNLITG	RUSTLING	Soft fluttering or crackling sounds
TENNICA	ANCIENT	Very old
TACCSARAT	CATARACTS	Opacities of the eye lens or capsule
DSEEPAVR	PERVADES	Spreads throughout
FELLAHIF	HALF-LIFE	Time for half of nuclei to radioactively decay
CICERSHNAA	SACCHARINE	Sweet
SUOLIBOIV	OBLIVIOUS	Unaware of
GFLUSHIFN	SHUFFLING	Sliding feet along the floor
ETHILSOUET	SILHOUETTE	Outline or profile
JASOLEU	JEALOUS	Envious
OPNOS	SNOOP	One who pries secretly
YESTIRTIL	STERILITY	Incapability of producing offspring
SIREHOFIR	HORRIFIES	Scares; shocks; causes horror
OATMUTIN	MUTATION	A change, as in nature, form, or quality
DECNAUTTACE	ACCENTUATED	Stressed; accented
ASSPG	GASPS	Sharp breaths
YESACLITHR	HYSTERICAL	Having excessive or uncontrollable emotion
YNABEMOG	BOGEYMAN	A terrifying presence; hobgoblin
MEGASUMR	RUMMAGES	Makes a disorderly search of
VEERN	NERVE	Brazen boldness
MORANUISAT	SANATORIUM	A place of convalescence from illness
BOOTHIRSSM	THROMBOSIS	Blood clot in blood vessel or heart
UPUONINOCSICS	INCONSPICUOUS	Not readily noticeable
ASUTFECOF	UFFOCATE	Kill by preventing access to oxygen
OSSNIVOCNUL	CONVULSIONS	Intense involuntary muscular contractions

Vocabulary Juggle Letter Game page 2

TRAVSEBI	VIBRATES	Shakes or trembles
PADRVOESNEGIP	EAVESDROPPING	Listening secretly
CNUTSAEUTP	PUNCTUATES	Emphasizes
TSSIIREN	SINISTER	Threatening evil
TOOCEPMITIN	COMPETITION	Others capable of winning
LONO	LOON	One who is crazy or simple-minded
PEDMRAIMOHGE	MIMEOGRAPHED	Copied
SIOVUIC	VICIOUS	Savage; evil; dangerous
PEXTAREESA	EXASPERATE	Make angry or impatient
REEBKRS	BERSERK	Deranged; crazed
HIPETCAT	PATHETIC	Arousing sympathy and compassion
GUMS	SMUG	Self-satisfied; complacent
MOATYAN	ANATOMY	Structure of an organism or organ
SUYSVRE	SURVEYS	Examines; looks at comprehensively
RGSRGEIT	TRIGGERS	Precipitates; causes to happen
CNALMHYEILCA	MECHANICALLY	Like a machine
MOCECESNM	COMMENCES	Starts
LERTMBE	TREMBLE	Shake violently

www.ingramcontent.com/pod-product-compliance
Lightning Source LLC
Chambersburg PA
CBHW051415070526
44584CB00023B/3432